D0190921

Montana
CURIOSITIES

Quirky characters,
roadside oddities &
other offbeat stuff

Ednor Therriault

Guilford, Connecticut

The prices, rates, and hours listed in this guidebook were confirmed at press time. We recommend, however, that you call establishments to obtain current information before traveling.

To buy books in quantity for corporate use or incentives, call **(800) 962–0973** or e-mail **premiums@GlobePequot.com.**

Photos by Ednor Therriault unless otherwise noted.
Maps by Sue Murray © Morris Book Publishing, LLC
Text design: Bret Kerr
Layout artist: Casey Shain
Project editor: John Burbidge

Library of Congress Cataloging-in-Publication Data

Therriault, Ednor.
  Montana curiosities : quirky characters, roadside oddities & other offbeat stuff / Ednor Therriault.
      p. cm.
  Includes index.
  ISBN 978-0-7627-4302-5
  1. Montana—Miscellanea. 2. Montana—Guidebooks. 3. Curiosities and wonders—Montana. I. Title.
  F731.6.T47 2010
  978.6—dc22

                                                                           2010005754

Printed in the United States of America

10 9 8 7 6 5 4 3 2 1

For Barbara McNew, in loving memory

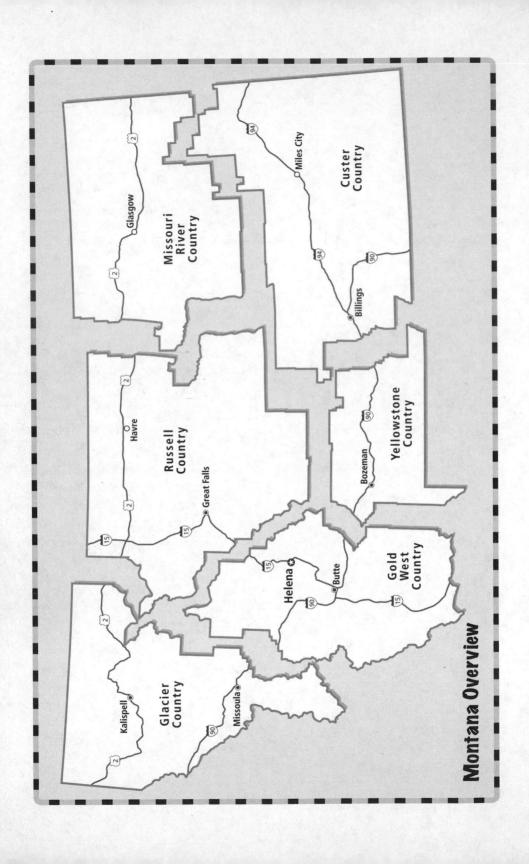

Montana Overview

contents

★ ★

acknowledgments

I'd like to thank Allen Jones, who became a fan of my humor blog and subsequently offered me the chance to write this book. His guidance, advice, good humor, and patience were invaluable, and I owe Allen a great debt of gratitude.

I'd also like to thank Erin Turner and John Burbidge of Globe Pequot Press. They're consummate pros whose steady hands helped guide me through the process of arranging an ungodly amount of raw information.

The hundreds of Montanans I interviewed while researching this book also deserve my thanks. They gave me their time, their patience, and lots of great quotes. Their honesty and willingness to share information with this nosey writer made the whole project possible. I wish I could give a free book to everyone who wanted one, but I'm using those for Christmas gifts.

Thanks to Kent Brothers Automotive for keeping my vehicles humming properly as I logged over 8,000 miles in six months, all within the borders of Montana. Sorry about all the dead bugs on the grille.

Thanks to all my friends and associates who chipped in with ideas for entries and their knowledge of various far-flung regions in Montana. You can only find out so much on the Internet. And thanks for the occasional place to crash.

Finally, I give my wholehearted thanks to my wife, Shannon, and my kids, Hudson and Sophia. You were great, intrepid traveling companions on some of my fact-finding junkets, and I really appreciate all of the creative ideas all three of you had for entries in the book. Thank you, also, for your patience and understanding as the deadline approached and I became more and more difficult to live with ("Go away! Daddy needs to write!").

introduction

When the U.S. government plopped down $15 million in 1803 for the Louisiana Purchase, they were mainly interested in the port of New Orleans on the Mississippi River. But what the heck, said France, for a few extra bucks and two states to be named later, we'll throw in a ton of uncharted territory. So with the stroke of a quill, the size of our country immediately doubled. But what about all that unseen real estate? We got the pink slip without ever kicking the tires or looking under the hood.

Enter Lewis and Clark. Thomas Jefferson sent the Corps of Discovery out West, to see if there was a reasonable Northwest Passage to the Pacific and maybe a good place for Jefferson to park his trailer and aboveground pool when he retired. On April 29, 1805, the intrepid explorers entered what is now Montana. They were amazed at the beauty of the landscape, the unusual variety of plants and trees, and the sheer volume of wildlife, from bison and antelope to grizzly bears and the odd two-headed calf.

Now, more than 200 years later, Montanans still tread the Lewis and Clark trail, still enthralled by the stunning beauty and breathtaking wildlife of the nation's fourth-biggest state. We've got a larger variety of mammals than any other state, to the point where roadkill is a significant part of our car insurance coverage. From Flathead Lake, the largest natural freshwater lake west of the Mississippi River, to Fort Peck Dam, the largest earthen dam in the world, Montana likes it large.

And fortunately for us fans of the strange and interesting, Montana also likes it weird. From the Barstool Races in February to the Pancake Races in May, from the Running of the Sheep in Reed Point to the Floating Flotilla in Twin Bridges, Montanans are no slackers when it comes to celebrating the absurd. You'll also find enough interesting, wacked-out characters out here to fill a caravan of clown cars.

The spirit of the Wild West still flows in our blood, and we aren't afraid to wear our weirdnesses on our rolled-up sleeves. So join me on this twisted trip through the Big Sky state, and take a tour of the freaky, the funny, and the downright curious people, places, and things that Montana has to offer.

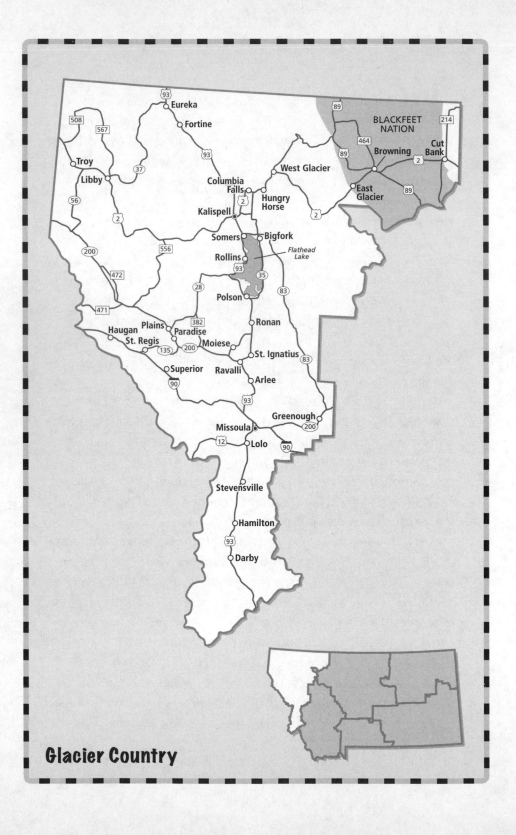

Glacier Country

Glacier Country

The northwestern chunk of Montana, with the Mission Range, the Seeley-Swans, and Glacier Park itself, is the most rugged, mountainous part of the state. From the giant cement penguin in Cut Bank, the coldest spot in the nation, to Hot Springs, where the tub in your hotel room fills with slimy, sulphurous hot spring water, Glacier Country has some of the wildest and weirdest curiosities that Montana has to offer.

If you're willing to dig deeper than the mainstream attractions of Glacier Park and Flathead Lake, you'll encounter some of Montana's biggest oddballs, from Missoula's Mushroom Guy to Polson's Flathead Monster. A heavy concentration of ski areas in Glacier Country attracts skiers and snowboarders, a segment of the population that tends toward unbalanced behavior. Witness the gelande competition at Missoula's Snowbowl, where the skier who jumps the farthest wins the privilege of taking one last jump—naked.

Glacier Park itself is surrounded by a ring of curiosities, from Columbia Falls to Browning. If you're visiting the park, by all means take the time to explore these smaller towns and check out some of the oddities listed here. It'll round out your trip to one of the most breathtaking national parks in the country.

Goofy Golf? This is Downright Deranged
Arlee

Along US 93 North, between Evaro and Arlee, there's a golf course you can play for free. Was it designed by Jack Nicklaus? No, more like Jack Nicholson. When he was the Joker in *Batman*. And it's miniature golf; Orange Acre Cars offers goofy golf at its goofiest.

Arranged throughout the property inhabited by the roadside used car lot, this ever-expanding putt-putt course is a wild-and-wooly homemade wonder. The putting surfaces are made up of a variety of shag carpet, and the tee boxes are actually car floor mats stapled to the wooden platform. Golfers contend with obstacles made from two-by-fours, upturned plastic planters, window shutters, and snake-

Find your center, be the ball. And watch out for those nails!

like curls of ribbed PVC pipe. As mini golf courses go, these holes are somewhat short. But what they lack in length, they make up for in bizarre construction and devious challenges.

One hole actually incorporates an ancient fiberglass outboard run-about that has a large silver skull and crossbones spray-painted across its bow. Another hole drops off the car lot office's deck, sending the ball through a pachinko-like series of ramps and bumpers on its way to the hole.

"We're always adding more holes," says Jeff Halverson, proprietor of Orange Acre Cars. He started building the funky mini golf course in 2008, with the help of volunteers. They use mostly recycled materials, and their creativity is downright devilish. Holes in one are rare.

Halverson, who is also the ambassador for a couch-surfing network based in Missoula, points out that the golf course is a great way to get visitors together to craft new holes and just to have fun. He hopes to one day have the course expanded to thirty-two holes. "Golf is physics. It's all about momentum and motion and gravity. It's also a neat way to meet people."

Orange Acre Cars is just a few miles north of the Mule Palace near Evaro, on US 93 North.

Warriors of the Wrecking Yard
Blackfeet Nation

When entering the Blackfeet reservation from any of the four directions, you'll drive under the proud, watchful gaze of two Indian warriors on horseback. You'll have to pull over, though, and get up close to these sculptures to see that they're cleverly crafted from scraps of rusted vehicles, bits of barbed wire, and the stones of an old mission school.

The statues are the work of Blackfeet tribal member Jay Laber. But this is a far cry from junkyard artistry. Laber has chosen materials that have significance to events in Blackfeet tribal history. The bases were made using recycled sandstone blocks from the Holy Family Mission,

built in the late 1800s on the Two Medicine River. The warriors themselves are constructed of parts gleaned from cars and trucks that
were destroyed in the massive flood of June 8, 1964.

Laber doesn't sketch his projects in advance. He says, "If I don't
sketch it, it's what it wants to be when it's done."

Located in scenic turnouts off either US 2 or US 89, each pair of
warriors can be appreciated year-round.

I wonder if this sculpture is covered by the standard
30,000-mile drivetrain warranty.

★ ★

Cowboys and Indians for Grown-Ups
Browning

Most folks will blow right through the Blackfeet reservation town of Browning on their way to Glacier Park, but if they do they're missing a great opportunity to witness some fascinating examples of frontier days history from the area. And I'm not talking about the concrete espresso tipi.

Right across the street from that cultural icon is the Diamond R Brown Cowboy Museum. You can't miss it, really, with its covered wagons and carts and random western paraphernalia piled up around the building. Ed Anderson started the museum in 2000, and named it after his great-great-grandfather, a bullwhacker who shipped freight from Great Falls and Helena in the late 1800s. Diamond R, as he was known, also served as a model for renowned western painter Charles M. Russell in several of his works.

Another well-known western artist, sculptor Bob Scriver from right here in Browning, is represented with several pieces in the museum. It's an eclectic collection that's constantly changing, as Ed spends the winters going to auctions and estate sales, always on the lookout for vintage cowboy gear. "Collecting cowboy stuff," he says, "you just get a fever for it. Like rodeo."

Ed was an outfitter in the area for twenty years, all the while feeding his jones for collecting cowboy (and Indian) stuff. And he knows rodeo—his grandmother's ranch produced Descent, widely considered to be the greatest bucking horse of all time.

A walk through his museum provides one surprising discovery after another, not all of them having to do with cowpokes and range riders. A huge moose rack (with an $800 price tag) greets you when you walk through the front doors. There are display cases full of spurs, stirrups, bits, and other ancient tack. You'll see authentic Indian moccasins and breastplates, and lots of handcrafted jewelry.

One of his most recent acquisitions is a stunning ammonite fossil, a fifty-pound specimen from Canada. It's 2 feet across, and even under a thick layer of dust this flattened Nautilus shell displays all the colors of the northern lights. It's just another little surprise you can uncover in the Diamond R Brown Cowboy Museum. Giddyup.

The Diamond R Brown Cowboy Museum is located on US 2 in Browning. They're open during the summer months. Call (406) 338-7413 for information.

You Sure This Isn't the Pony Espresso?
Browning

One of the coolest roadside attractions in Montana is also one of the oldest. For pure, old-school highway kitsch, you can't beat the concrete tipi espresso stand in Browning.

At 50 feet tall, this iconic cone is quite a bit larger than your regulation tipi. Built in 1934 by Robert Kramer, the tipi was originally a gas station where travelers could fill up their Hudsons, and hungry workers and tourists heading for Glacier Park could pick up a light lunch. Kramer's Wigwam, as it was known, was moved shortly after it was built in order to make room for a new hospital.

The tipi has also served as a café and coffee shop over the years, and eventually fulfilled its destiny by becoming the first espresso stand in Browning. Famed local sculptor Bob Scriver bought the tipi and moved it to its current location, on US 2 near the middle of town.

While you're waiting inside this peripatetic tipi for the kid behind the counter to whip up your half-caf mochaccino, you can browse through a variety of handcrafted jewelry, beaded moccasins, and other native art. Just don't ask for a table in the corner.

Gypsy's Espresso is on the east side of US 2 (for now) in Browning, across from the Diamond R Brown Cowboy Museum.

It's been around longer than any
espresso stand you know of.

★ ★

When You Enter the Next Level of Reality, Please Wipe Your Feet
Columbia Falls

What would you do if you were walking through a forest in north-west Montana, and you suddenly realized that the trees were all growing in spirals, and tilted in the same direction? Why, you'd build a funhouse on the hillside, of course, and charge people $8 to come inside and "Feel the Power of Nature."

The Montana Vortex and House of Mystery, just a couple of miles east of Columbia Falls, is a little hokey, kind of funky, and a little New Age woo-woo. In short, it's the perfect Montana Curiosity! And it's so much more than a freaky, slanted house full of illusions. Native Americans first discovered the weird area where the trees grew funny, and people have been seeing odd things here ever since. In 1970 the place was officially established as a vortex, and the House of Mystery was built.

The site actually has three vortexes, which are powerful spirals of magnetic energy, tangled up with each other. The largest, at 216 feet in diameter, can actually cause you to feel a bit dizzy when you stand in the very center. Several displays and activities are scattered throughout the wooded hillside, where visitors can see their own

Trivia

Browning holds the record for the biggest temperature change in twenty-four hours. They went from 44 degrees above zero to minus 56 on January 25 and 26, 1916. That's what happens when everyone in town turns off their furnaces at exactly the same moment.

We have liftoff.

auras, watch their height change as the vortex "shrinks their atoms," and step through the Golden Door into an alternate reality.

Make sure you take the guided tour so you don't miss any of the fun. The House of Mystery is not much of a mystery, really, but a clever collection of optical illusions that are a lot of fun to witness. And it definitely makes for some great photo opportunities.

Bring an open mind and a camera, and you could easily spend half a day taking in the strange energy and mind-bending illusions. As you walk from the gift shop through the Portal, the disclaimer above the door says it all: "Management Is Not Responsible For World View Changes."

Montana Vortex and House of Mystery is located about 2 miles east of Columbia Falls, on US 2 East. They are open during the summer months. Call (406) 892-1210 or visit www.montanavortex.com.

★ ★

They're Into the Whole Brevity Thing
Columbia Falls

If you're looking for the smallest bowling alley in Montana, you just may find it in Columbia Falls. Glacier Lanes boasts a mere eight standard bowling lanes—typical bowling centers usually have at least three times that.

Of the fifty or so bowling alleys in Montana, only one, the Stockman Lanes in Circle, has fewer lanes. But they also have a separate restaurant and lounge, whereas the Glacier Lanes handles all that business in the same large room as the bowling alleys. Many find that the more intimate confines make for a more enjoyable bowling experience.

Yes, they have ten-pound balls.

Trivia

Triple Divide Peak in Glacier Park is the only place in the world where the melting snow feeds rivers that flow to three different oceans: the Pacific, the Arctic, and the Atlantic. I know what every guy who reads this is going to try to do when he gets up there.

The alley was opened in 1961 by Tom Smith, and is still a popular local hangout. There are usually at least one or two lanes active, and more on weekends and in the summer. Things really heat up in the fall when they host a Bowl for Kids Sake event, which raises funds for the Flathead Big Brothers and Big Sisters group.

So if you find yourself in the North Flathead Valley and your inner Lebowski wants to bowl a few frames without having to deal with the crowds and impersonal service of a giant Bowl-a-Rama—type center, slide in to the Glacier Lanes and lace up a pair of rentals. Unless, of course, it's a Saturday and you don't roll on Shabbos.

Glacier Lanes is at 307 Nucleus Avenue in Columbia Falls. Call (406) 892-5858 for more information.

Say, Neighbor, Can I Borrow a Cup of Honey?
Columbia Falls

She was a free-spirited flower child, floating on the summer wind through the Flathead Valley in a hand-painted Volkswagen bug. He was a hard-working, fun-loving, down-to-earth type with a similar love of flowers and a yen for travel. Perhaps they were destined to meet, these two star-crossed campers.

When he hooked his tiny travel trailer to her flower-covered Beetle, it was a cosmic connection that joined two disparate lives forever.

You can still see them there, Huck the bear and his VW sweetie, 8 feet above the earth, welcoming travelers to the Glacier Peaks RV Park. Huck is gracious as ever, holding open the door to his trailer with a hearty, "Hi, neighbor!"

To say hello to Huck, look for Glacier Peaks RV Park, located on MT 40, just west of Columbia Falls.

A Beetle pulling a trailer? That's about as likely as a talking bear.

★ ★

Am I Drunk, Or Is That a Giant Penguin?
Cut Bank

Between I-15 and East Glacier, you can drive right up to the Holy
Grail of Montana Curiosities. This 27-foot-tall cement penguin greets
you as you enter Cut Bank from the east on US 2. And I mean this
literally: The penguin talks (sometimes).

That's the author, on the lower right.
He's not particularly tall,
but the bird is.

★ ★

Constructed of cement over a metal frame and weighing over five tons, the black-and-white penguin in a bright red toque stands in front of the Glacier Gateway Inn. The adjacent parking lot gives plenty of room for a variety of photo opportunities, including the popular, "look, I'm holding the giant penguin in the palm of my hand" gag.

The penguin was built by hotel owner Ron Gustafson in 1989, and the 6-foot-tall base explains why: "Welcome to Cut Bank, Coldest Spot in the Nation." That's also the phrase continually spoken by the penguin through a speaker in the base (if it's not on the fritz). This boast may be fightin' words, though, to the frigid folk in Stanley, Idaho, which regularly records the coldest average temp in the lower forty-eight. But, alas, Stanley lacks a giant flightless bird. Especially one that talks (when it's working).

The Cut Bank Penguin is just off the road when you enter Cut Bank from the east on US 2. You can't miss it. Seriously. If you do, maybe you should let someone else drive while you take a nap.

The Biggest Little Museum in the Bitterroot
Darby

The oldest structure in Darby is also its most interesting. The Pioneer Memorial Museum is contained in a 20-foot by 45-foot log cabin, originally built in 1886 on nearby Tin Cup Creek, two years before Darby was founded.

Under the moss-covered roof, you'll find hundreds of treasures and artifacts on display. Curators from the local historical society have managed to cram 150 years of pioneer life into a space no bigger than your average Starbuck's.

There are Indian artifacts from nearby Lake Como, including tools made from river rocks and arrowheads crafted from shale and obsidian. Mostly, though, it's the trappings and necessities of the white settler on display here, and some items indicate a surprisingly sophisticated lifestyle for people who had never even seen two-ply toilet paper.

★ ★

An intricate wedding dress from 1903 hangs smartly on a mannequin frame, and other female finery is arranged around it, suggesting
a refinement that seems out of place with our image of the rough-
and-tumble prairie lifestyle. Music played a big part of that lifestyle,
and like most small-town pioneer museums, this one has a fully
restored vintage organ. It's a beautiful Peloubet & Co. instrument,
and it even features some interesting sheet music: "Take Your Girlie
to the Movies (If You Can't Make Love at Home)."

The gold rush that first brought white settlers to the area is represented, with gold pans, miner's picks, and ancient cooking utensils

"Oh, Mary, I love what you've done with the living room!
The other pioneer wives will be so jealous."

★ ★

and vessels. Coffee grinders, whiskey jugs, and medicine bottles are there to remind us of what kept the miners going.

One of the most unique items on display is at the back end of the museum, in a corner filled with schoolhouse gear and a knitting machine. It's a large map of the U.S., circa 1906. It seems to be the classroom type that the teacher would pull down in front of the blackboard. Well, back when they had blackboards anyway. The map was made before Hawaii and Alaska joined the union, of course, so those states are not visible (whereas you can see them on most modern maps, just off the coast of Texas).

The Darby Pioneer Memorial Museum is just behind the Town Hall, in the city park in downtown Darby, on US 93 South. Donations are accepted.

Hat's Off to the Hat Man
Darby

When John Wayne's stunt double, Jim Burk, needed a cowboy hat, he didn't just buy one off the rack, pilgrim. No ma'am, he went to see the Hat Man in Darby.

Primo cowboy hats are the specialty at the Double H Custom Hat Company, owned and operated by Jimmy Harrison, known around these parts as "Jimmy the Hat Man."

And it's not just Burk, the simulated Duke, who buys his hats from Jimmy, either. The Hat Man has made custom lids for the likes of Garth Brooks, Terri Clark, Mark Chestnutt, Tanya Tucker, and Willie Nelson, to name just a few. He even made a white felted beaver hat for former President George W. Bush, complete with an inlaid eagle on the crown.

"I enjoy individualizing 'em," says Jimmy. "I very seldom make the same hat twice." He does perform the occasional duplicate, however, when he's asked to re-create the John Wayne–style hat or Tom Selleck's "Quigley" hat or the Dwight Yoakam number the country star can be seen peeking out from under on nearly all his album covers.

✦ ✦

If you want to know how the metric system nearly ruined
the ten-gallon hat, ask Jimmy the Hat Man.

Born and raised in Dillon, Jimmy learned the hat trade from a master hatter in Wisdom after getting busted up riding in the rodeo. He's been in the Darby area for about fifteen years, and is most famous locally for donating the official cowboy hat to the winner of the Miss Montana Rodeo competition each year. "I let the winner design her own hat," he says, pointing at a signed photo of a previous rodeo queen wearing a felted beaver hat with a cowhide brim, the rodeo-queen tiara clamped to the crown.

He also makes a few palm-leaf hats, but don't expect to walk in and pluck one off the shelf for the same price as a steak dinner. Jimmy politely but firmly tells budget-minded customers that the local ranch supply store has plenty of cheap, straw cowboy hats. His custom-made works of art can run to over $2,000.

Jimmy enjoys running his shop in downtown Darby, which is taking on more and more of a frontier days, western look in its

★ ★

Trivia

The tallest known ponderosa pine in the state is near Fish Creek
Road, just west of Alberton off I-90. It stands 194 feet tall and is 78
inches in diameter at the base. And no, it didn't play basketball in
high school, but thanks for asking.

architecture and attitude. "I like meeting new and interesting people
every day," he says. "It makes it a pleasure."

He also crafts top hats, bowlers, homburgs, and derbies, but to
wear one of those fancy-pants hats on the boardwalks of Darby
would take some true grit.

Double H Custom Hat Company is located at 121 South Main
Street, on US 93 South in Darby. Call 1-877-HAT-MAKR or visit
www.doublehhats.com.

A Giant Purple Spoon Points the Way to Glacier Park
East Glacier

"What's the point of having a 14-foot spoon in your front yard if it's
not purple?" It's hard to argue with logic like that, especially when it
comes from Jo Wagner, owner of the World's Largest Purple Spoon
(maybe) in East Glacier.

It's the perfect utensil for a swimming pool full of Frosted Flakes,
but where would you see that outside of a Disney movie? This spoon
has only one function, and it's to call attention to its smaller brethren, Jo's hand-carved wooden spoons.

The Spiral Spoon on MT 49 in East Glacier features beautiful,
hand-carved wooden spoons that have been lovingly crafted by Jo

If you have a purple spoon that's
bigger than this, call me.

since 1999. She uses some fifty types of wood, from koa and maple to more exotic woods like lignum vitae, a rock-hard tradewood that actually sinks in water. After several rounds of sanding and submersion in water to bring out the grain, the spoons eventually are soaked in "Spiral Spoon snake oil" to make them kitchen tough and near-impervious to stains. And Jo usually carves a leaf into the handle, with its stem spiraling around from bowl to tip.

The giant purple spoon also sports the trademark leaf, with its stem carefully wrapped around the handle. The big spoon's genesis is rooted in the problem of how to dispose of the fine sawdust created by the sanding of the wooden spoons. Jo says she came up with a type of papier-mâché, mixing the sawdust with newspaper and water. The spoon was shaped with the sawdust mixture, and a skin was created out of newspaper.

The particular shade of purple, she says, is called aubergine, which is a type of eggplant. When she and her husband, Charley, were trying to decide on a pet name for the spoon, Jo figured that the only person she knew of who would actually use the word "aubergine" was Martha Stewart. So the Largest Purple Spoon in the World (maybe) is known as Big Martha. It's a good thing.

The World's Largest Purple Spoon (maybe) is right out front at the Spiral Spoon, 1012 MT 49 in East Glacier. Try calling (406) 226-4558 or pay a visit to www.thespiralspoon.com.

Double the Bullets, Double Your Fun!
Eureka

Sometimes you'll hear a story or witness an event that is so freaky, so unlikely, that it takes some time and effort (and maybe an adult beverage or two) to wrap your mind around it.

One such occurrence is documented and displayed in the Tobacco Valley Historical Village in Eureka. In an unassuming little display box, laid out under glass, is the evidence and account of this one-in-a-million shot. Or, more accurately, two-in-a-million.

★ ★

The year was 1881 and Joe Fredrickson was working in a lumber camp on the Tobacco Plains. Fredrickson and his friend, Jack Hardy, left the camp to hunt some meat. Fredrickson spied a deer on top of a ridge, and dropped it with a single shot.

He rushed up the hill to claim his prize, only to meet Hardy walking up from the other side. "I made a fine shot," he said to Hardy. But the other man claimed he had shot the deer, and the two began to argue over who actually had made the kill. They finally used their satellite phone to call in some CSI techs to do a ballistics and DNA analysis on the carcass. Not really. What they did was drag the deer back to camp where the cook performed an autopsy, uh, I mean

It's not often you get to see the evidence of a one-in-a-million shot.

★ ★

dressed it out. She cut open the heart of the animal, and there, to everyone's astonishment, she found two lead bullets fused together. The men had both pulled the trigger at the same moment, and the slugs had met in the heart and joined together. Both men immediately ran into town to buy lottery tickets.

Now, more than one hundred years later, the fused bullets are displayed under glass in the little case, lying next to a buckskin pouch

The Flathead's Homegrown Radio Station

If you're driving, boating, or hiking anywhere in the Flathead Valley and you find yourself wishing for a nonstop stream of great music, you're in luck. The Montana Radio Café, broadcast from Scott Johnston's front porch in Creston, stands ready to fulfill your musical desires.

The tiny, one-hundred-watt FM station resides at 101.9 on the dial, but is also streamed worldwide on the Internet at www .montanaradiocafe.org. The coverage of the radio signal varies, but according to Johnston, folks have reportedly been able to tune in as far south as Arlee and as far north as Whitefish and beyond.

"I love music," says Johnston about his passion for the station. After spending years working in commercial radio, he became frustrated and bored with the increasingly narrow classifications and mind-numbing repetition of standard FM programming. "I thought, what if somebody just played good music? Would it make it?"

Since going on-air in 2004, it has done just that. With an eclectic play list of more than 20,000 songs, Montana Radio Café has sponsors from all over the Flathead Valley, and supporters from all that was made from that very deer. The rest of the museum is worth a look, too, with its schoolhouse, church, and library. But when you look at the two lead bullets that were plucked from that deer's heart, it's difficult to comprehend the odds of such a thing actually happening.

Eureka's Tobacco Valley Historical Village is located at 4 Dewey Avenue. They can be reached at (406) 297-7654.

over the globe. Working with other music-minded volunteers, Johnston also puts on occasional concerts at the KM Theatre in nearby Kalispell.

Musicians periodically drop by to set a spell and do some picking on the front porch with Johnston, an accomplished guitarist. He keeps the transmitter and servers and other bulky hardware in his basement, which enables him to maintain an uncluttered, inviting front porch. It's enclosed, of course, protecting him from the elements while he broadcasts music by thousands of artists both famous and obscure. You can hear B.B. King, Delbert McClinton, Bruce Cockburn, and Gillian Welch, as well as lesser-known artists like the Badgers, or Montana favorites like John Floridis and Shane Clouse. But you'll have to go online to see who's playing, because Johnston doesn't clutter up the flow with lengthy announcing. He does mention his sponsors frequently, though, in a down-home, "Tell 'em Scott sent ya" kind of way.

The studio is easy to find on MT 35 between Bigfork and Columbia Falls. Look for the hundred-foot transmitter tower rising into the sky, next to the classic farmhouse with the neon "On Air" sign blazing proudly in the front porch window for all to see.

For more information, visit www.montanaradiocafe.org.

★ ★

Concrete Indians Not Included
Flathead Lake

If you drive south from Bigfork on MT 35, look to the right as you approach Woods Bay and you'll see what appears to be the nose of a Saturn Five rocket emerging from the earth. Don't panic! It's not a moon shot, it's just the Concrete Tipi.

Evidently built as a kitschy homage to the Native Americans in the area, this unique structure has been on the lakeshore since the 1970s. Three stories high and tipped in brown paint, these days the Concrete Tipi is pretty run down. The paint has mostly peeled off, but you can still see evidence of decorative, Indian-style illustrations here and there.

It doesn't seem to be inhabited currently, but it is crammed full of someone's junk. As a family home, the Tipi would obviously present many challenges, one of which would be this: What would a kid do when she misbehaves and is told to go stand in the corner?

The Concrete Tipi is located just north of Woods Bay on MT 35, on the east side of Flathead Lake. It's not open to the public.

Stonehenge, Where the Demons Dwell . . .
Fortine

If you've got a hankering to see Stonehenge, you can hop a plane to Wiltshire, England, and eat boiled food for a week. Go ahead, ask your restaurant server for an English muffin—they never heard of 'em!

Or you can save yourself a lot of time and money by simply taking a little detour off US 93 near Fortine, where a wealthy recluse has installed a replica of the mysterious monument on his private golf course. And unlike the tiny version that was in danger of being crushed by a dwarf in *Spinal Tap,* this replica is full-size.

I spoke briefly to the owner, who was gracious enough to allow me to walk around his Stonehenge to snap a few photos. He is a very private person, however, and would not allow his name to be published. He also reminded me that the golf course was a private facility, on private property. He dodged most of my questions about when he built it, what techniques were used, and what kind of stones they were. He wouldn't even give me his real name. In fact, the only detail I could pry out of him was the inspiration for the monument's construction.

"It all boils down to this," he said, indicating the glass of white wine he was drinking. Obviously, he's got to have a sense of humor

Just one of the graceful curves and intricate constructions you'll find at Stonehenge, Montana.

to put the time and considerable expense into designing and constructing a full-scale duplicate of the 4,500-year-old stone edifice.

A system of spotlights illuminates the monument at night, and
it must be pretty impressive then, because in the daylight it is overwhelming. Some of the lateral stones, or lintels, laid atop two vertical
stones are about 25 feet tall. The massive bulk of these cream-
colored stones makes you wonder about what it took to get them
there, on a manicured fairway overlooking a beautiful island par-3
on this private eighteen-hole golf course. But like the original Stonehenge, it looks like this replica will keep its secrets.

A glimpse of Montana's Stonehenge can be had from Crystal Lake
Road off US 93 near Fortine. You can drive past the golf course, close
enough to view the monument. The golf course is private property,
though, and trespassing is a violation of the law.

You Should See the Guy Who Milks It
Greenough/Ovando

According to official traffic counts, nearly 10,000 vehicles a day drive
past the Clearwater Junction, where MT 83 juts off MT 200 and the
Clearwater River dumps into the Blackfoot. Many people passing by
pay little attention to the gargantuan sentinel standing on a trailer
at the junction, but a few first-timers always do a fierce double take
when they see the Stoney's giant cow.

Trivia

**Melting snow creates 70 percent of Montana's stream flow. The
other 30 percent probably comes from guys peeing on Triple Divide
Peak.**

"When I moo, people listen."

Standing some 14 feet tall and longer than your average panel truck, the bovine behemoth is a well-known landmark that serves a valuable purpose for anyone giving directions in the area. Going from Missoula to Seeley? Easy—drive up the Blackfoot River on MT 200, turn left at the giant cow. Making your way from Glacier Park to Bonner? Piece of cake. Head south on 83, hang a right at the giant cow.

"If we take it out of here for a parade or something, people get lost. 'Where's the cow?'" laughs Ken Price, the owner of Stoney's Kwik Stop, the name of which is emblazoned on the side of the giant beast. He says the cow (which, upon closer inspection, proves to be a, uh, male cow) has been on the spot for over forty years, since it was purchased for $5,000 by the original owner, Bud Lake.

There's usually a group of curiosity-seekers, especially in the summer, gathered around the fiberglass cow to take some touristy photos. The cow/bull, though, gazes contentedly into the distance with its volleyball-size eyes of blue, silently enduring the embarrassing poses and lurid comments of the passing tourists.

Travelers will come and go, but the giant cow of Clearwater Junction holds its ground. The cow abides.

You can't miss the giant cow at the junction of MT 83 and MT 200.

Hamilton's Hollow Skyscraper
Hamilton

If you drive into Hamilton from the north on US 93, you'll see a large smokestack come into view before you even cross the Bitterroot River. As you get closer, you'll note that a large "R" is attached to the top of the stack. You can try asking the locals what the "R" stands for, but you'll most likely get answers ranging from Ritalin factory to roadkill Mecca. But the real answer is far more interesting.

Welcome to the Riverside stack. You might be able to guess the name when you see the Riverside Convenience Store and Riverside Lawn Implements at its base, near the Bitterroot River. The true story of the smokestack's origin is fraught with big dreams and broken promises. And sugar beets.

The 85-foot tower was built in 1917 as part of the Montana-Utah Sugar Company's proposed beet processing plant, which was never completed. Big plans were made, bonds were sold to finance the construction, and forty tons of Russian beet seeds were planted

Montana is the name of an indie pop band in Australia. Down under, your unwanted relatives invade your home during the winter, not the summer.

The "R" stands for, "Really, really tall."

in the fertile soil of the Bitterroot Valley. Manpower was scarce on account of the war, so local schoolchildren were paid $1.50 a day to tend the crops.

The war drove up steel prices, however, until the processing plant was $200,000 over budget before the buildings were even constructed on the land that had been donated by the Anaconda Copper Company. Footings were poured, but when the financing fell through, all construction was halted. The beet crop was harvested

Hamilton's Favorite Son

The last scene of *The Big Chill* delivers a satisfying sucker punch when Three Dog Night starts singing, "Jeremiah was a bullfrog . . ." The reunited baby boomers begin laughing and joking as if they'll never again have to think about their crushing mortgages, sagging bodies, or receding hairlines.

"Joy to the World" was the biggest hit written by the late Hoyt Axton, a well-loved resident of the Bitterroot Valley who passed away in 1999 at age sixty-one. The song spent six weeks at number one when it was originally released in 1971, and *Chill*'s soundtrack helped shine a little bit of spotlight back onto Axton, the one-time San Francisco folkie. He'd written other songs for successful artists, including "Greenback Dollar," which was a big hit for the Kingsmen. But "Joy to the World" remains his most well known work, as evidenced by all the frog-themed items people leave around his gravesite in Hamilton.

★ ★

and sold to a sugar company with a plant in nearby Missoula, and, as Tony Baretta used to say, that's the name of that tune.

The smokestack still stands today, nearly one hundred years later— a testament to wartime ambition, civic pride and optimism, and that unshakable, western can-do spirit.

And sugar beets.

The Riverside Smokestack is located on US 93 South, at the north end of Hamilton. You can't miss it.

He had a pretty good following performing his own material, with songs like "Boney Fingers" and "Della and the Dealer." Axton also had a successful acting career, playing a few memorable characters that allowed him to take advantage of his gruff, burly exterior. Among other roles, he was the chronically preoccupied inventor in *Gremlins,* and also played the amiable-but-shrewd sheriff in *Disorganized Crime*, a comic caper that was filmed in and around Hamilton.

Axton's sense of humor was on full display in that movie, and he was given a lot of memorable lines. One of my favorites is his reply to dispatch when they were checking in with him on a stakeout: "It's quieter than a foam rubber wind chime out there."

He didn't get all the musical talent in his family, incidentally. His mother, Mae Boren Axton, co-wrote "Heartbreak Hotel," the first hit for Elvis Presley.

Hoyt Axton's grave can be seen at Riverview Cemetery, just west of Hamilton on Westbridge Road.

★ ★

When You Leave This Museum, Check Yourself for Ticks
Hamilton

You think the ticks are big where you come from? How about the pair of pancake-size specimens on display in the Ravalli County Museum in Hamilton? Relax, they're not real. At thirty-two times their normal size, however, they are one of the more shiver-inducing displays in the Tick Room.

This museum is fairly typical of the small-town pioneer museums scattered throughout the state, with its collections of settler para-phernalia, Indian craftwork, and other stuff from the 1800s. But what really sets it apart is the Tick Room, which is dedicated to the Rocky Mountain Labs story of the spotted fever outbreak one hundred years ago.

Miners, settlers, trappers, and soldiers up and down the Bitterroot Valley started falling ill and dying from what they called the "black measles" or "blue disease." By some accounts, the mortality rate was as high as 77 percent. Oddly, the vast majority of the cases were occurring on only one side of the Bitterroot River. Symptoms of spot-ted fever include fever, headache, muscle pain, and nausea. Kind of like you feel after watching a Paulie Shore movie.

Researchers at the Rocky Mountain Laboratories worked to find a vaccine for the disease, and the organism that causes the infection was discovered to be a parasite found in ticks. The offending organ-ism, modestly named *Rickettsia rickettsii* by its discoverer, Howard T. Ricketts, is passed from ticks to mammals. Researchers injected sheep and mice with ground-up ticks to try and infect them, but instead the animals wound up developing an immunity to the disease. This quickly led to a vaccine and antibiotic to combat the disease. Unfor-tunately, six people died in the process, after they became infected and succumbed to the fever.

The Rocky Mountain Labs are still very much active in Hamilton, working on cures and vaccines for infectious diseases. But the Tick Room in the museum is a great way to learn the history of the labs

★ ★

and the whole fascinating, tragic story of the Rocky Mountain Spotted Fever.

Bonus creepiness: When you turn the big cylinder to rotate the oversize model ticks, it makes a really weird noise that sounds like it's coming from the ticks.

The Ravalli County Museum is located at 205 Bedford Street in Hamilton. Their hours are Tuesday through Friday, from 10 a.m. to 4 p.m., and Saturday from 9 a.m. to 1 p.m. They're closed Sunday and Monday. Call (406) 363-3338 or visit www.brvhsmuseum.org.

This Is One Crazy Coin Collection
Haugen

How far does a dollar go these days? At the 50,000 Silver Dollar Bar in Haugen, it goes all the way from the floor to the ceiling, and from one end of the bar clear to the other.

Known as the 10,000 Silver Dollar Bar until May of 2008, the giant restaurant/bar/casino/gift shop along I-90 has had so many silver dollars donated by people passing through that it had to change its name to keep up with the quantity. There are well over 50,000 dollar coins filling up the 30-foot-high walls, and 2,115 solid silver specimens are embedded in the long bar top. They're under a thick layer of clear acrylic, so don't get any ideas about prying out some gas money while you're there.

The very first dollar put into the bar top came from Gerry and Marie Lincoln in 1952, and the bar has been in the Lincoln family ever since. That might help explain the life-size wood carving of Honest Abe stationed at the entrance to the casino. Originally located in Cherry Springs near Alberton, Lincoln's Silver Dollar Bar was moved to Haugen in 1956, and then to a different location in Haugen in 1976.

Some 1,500 dollar coins are donated to the bar each year. The huge collection contains 10,623 genuine vintage silver dollars, and modern Eisenhower coins make up the rest. The oldest coin, an 1876 trade dollar from Hong Kong, is in the bar top near the west end.

★ ★

**If you laid every silver dollar in this bar end to
end, it would really upset the owners.**

As you stroll through the cavernous gift shop, you'll encounter
several sets of bull horns, stacks of cowboy hats, ornate swords,
knives, jewelry, beaded western belts, and a few mounted jackalope
heads. The jackalope, a mythical beast of the West, is a desert hare
sporting an impressive set of antlers. Like the hoop snake and the
side-hill wompus, the jackalope is a legendary critter that may or may
not exist outside the imagination of a skilled taxidermist.

The 50,000 Silver Dollar Bar is a must-see if you're traveling in
western Montana. They are located in Haugen, off exit 16 on I-90.
Call (406) 678-4242 if you get lost. Stop in and check it out before
they have to change the name again.

★ ★

Drinking and Driving Encouraged Here
Hungry Horse

If you think it's hard to keep your seat on a Martin City barstool, try doing it when the stool is moving at 20 miles per hour.

That's exactly what happens in the Martin City Barstool Races, during Cabin Fever Days in the Bad Rock Canyon each February. People from all over the Flathead area gather each year in this tiny northern hamlet to swill beer, blow off steam, and race ski-mounted barstools down a gently sloping Main Street right into the heart of town.

Volunteers with snowplows prep the 200-yard course by grooming the snow, which is never in short supply in this part of the state. Then they use backhoes to break up the ice chunks and back blade it to a relatively level racing surface. Meanwhile, drivers and pushers congregate in the South Fork Saloon to talk strategy. It's a lot like a NASCAR pit area, only instead of talking horsepower and drafting schemes, they're trading tips on what to use for a ski coating. One racer I spoke to swears by Pam cooking spray. "Original flavor," he said, "not the garlic."

The festival, which draws thousands of winter-weary fun seekers, features pool tournaments, a poker run, karaoke, live bands, Texas hold-em tournaments, and hot food from several street vendors. The winters are long and harsh in the Bad Rock Canyon, and Cabin Fever Days serves as a pressure valve that probably prevents this beautiful little corner of Montana from becoming the serial killer capital of the world.

The Barstool Races are the main event, of course, and contestants pay a $15 fee to enter their homemade contraptions. Money goes to the Canyon Quick Response Unit, the Head Start chapter, and to the local fire department. The first race was thirty years ago, and organizers quickly had to break down the racers into different divisions as imaginations ran wild and the actual barstool became less of a design element. Now these frostbitten speed freaks race in four categories: steerable, non-steerable, furniture, and the open division. You'll see

"What's that? Is this my crash helmet? Oh, I hope not . . ."

beds, pirate ships, flying saucers, giant beer bottles, and even a few purists riding barstools down the slope.

The crashes are spectacular. When riders lose control and slam their sleds into the hay bales that line the course, the spectators scatter. If the action gets too wild, revelers can always retreat to the saloon, where they'll find a stationary barstool or two.

Martin City is about 8 miles east of Columbia Falls on US 2. For more info, call the South Fork Saloon at (406) 387-9971.

★ ★

Does a Blue Cow Give Blue Milk?

Kalispell

If there's one thing Montana is lousy with, it's giant cow statues. From Clearwater Junction to Three Forks, these massive tributes to the dairy and beef industries dot the landscape like sloe-eyed sentries guarding our bucolic rural landscapes.

One of the newest bovine behemoths to startle drivers and attract curious motorists is Suds, the giant blue-and-black cow standing in the corner of the parking lot of Blue Cow Car Wash in Kalispell. Ten

"I tell ya, if it's not one thing, it's an udder! Yuk yuk. Moo."

feet tall and 12 feet long, Suds is a fearsome yet strangely soothing specimen, an oversize mascot for the new car wash.

The cow is an astonishingly detailed fiberglass likeness created by the Fiberglass Animals Shapes and Trademarks Company in Sparta, Wisconsin. According to owner Steve Gascoigne, Suds cost around $13,000, roughly six times the amount of your average dairy cow made of beef. Of course Suds won't produce any milk, in spite of her ice chest–size udder, realistic down to the huge veins that run up to her belly.

"We wanted something eye-catching," says Gascoigne, when asked why a cow. He says they chose the name for the car wash specifically with this big mascot in mind.

But wait, that's not all—step inside the soup café that shares the building with the car wash and you'll meet up with Suds's offspring: two matching blue-and-black calves as big as horses, and a third, smaller calf that is bisected by a kids' slide.

Beef, milk, mascot, playground equipment—it's no wonder we hold the ubiquitous and versatile cow in such high regard in Montana.

Blue Cow Car Wash is located at 10 Commons Way in Kalispell, just off US 93 North. Their phone number is (406) 755-6988.

Those Cowboy Boots Must Have a Hell of a Grip
Kalispell

He looks down over his shoulder at the busy traffic on Kalispell's Main Street. His gloved hands clutch a rope that holds him up on the second-story wall, above the Noice Art Gallery. Is he a mountain climber with a horrible sense of direction? Is he a second-story man making a getaway with a satchel full of stolen gems? Naw, he's just the climbing cowboy.

And he ain't even real, pardner. He's the creation of Kalispell artist Kay Lynn, and he's been stopping traffic on Main Street for a couple

★ ★

of years now. Why a cowboy? Why climbing a building? Well, you'd have to ask the artist. But she may be difficult to reach, as she is reportedly holed up in her studio, crafting a full-size horse to place on the building's roof.

The climbing cowboy is just above the Noice Art Gallery, at 127 Main Street in Kalispell.

"I don't know, Robin. I kind of prefer our
original costumes. Robin? Robin . . . ?"

★ ★

It's Where the Locals Go
Kalispell

If you pass through Kalispell without stopping at Sykes Grocery and Market, you'll be doing yourself a major disservice. Why, it would be like driving through Primm, Nevada, and not bothering to stop and see the Bonnie and Clyde Death Car.

The original home of the 10-cent cup of coffee (still available if you're over sixty-five or ordering food), Sykes is a unique experience that you just have to see for yourself. What began as a neighborhood grocery store over one hundred years ago is still a popular gathering spot for locals and in-the-know visitors. It is a grocery store, yes, but there's also a recently expanded pharmacy and a spacious, old-school diner.

Doug and Judy Wise ran Sykes from the 1950s until 2008, when they sold the store to Mike and Mary McFarland. The McFarlands, to the great relief of everyone in Kalispell, vowed to maintain the original look and feel of the venerated establishment.

Although they've put in new bathrooms and expanded the pharmacy, the rest of Sykes is just the way it has been for decades. Wood-paneled walls surround the restaurant, and the small grocery store still offers all kinds of comestibles stacked on sixty-year-old shelving fixtures. Diner tables are covered with dozens of local business ads, and hundreds of cattle brands are mounted high on the wall, running from one end of the building to the other.

The restaurant features a varied menu at reasonable prices, and you can sit at the long red soda fountain counter with twenty other people to enjoy your meal. The clam chowder they have on Friday is homemade, and it is excellent.

The old and the new mix it up throughout Sykes. An ATM machine shares floor space with ancient scales and check stands. Old-timers share tables with younger folks, sipping their 10-cent coffee and talking about everything under the sun.

★ ★

Kalispell's most beloved gathering place is the best spot to measure this lake town's zeitgeist. Like it says on the plaque near the front door, "Nobody goes away a stranger."

Sykes Grocery and Market is located at 202 Second Avenue West in Kalispell. Call (406) 257-4304.

Like a Sturgeon
Libby

If a sand shark mated with a bulldog, and somehow an armadillo got involved, the result would probably look like the white sturgeon. It may be butt-ugly, but it's also endangered, and the Kootenai River population is the only one naturally isolated from the lower Columbia River drainage. Man-made facilities and dams cut off the rest.

This big fish, also known as the Pacific sturgeon, has a face only a mother could love. Big, bony spines along its back and rows of cartilage plates along its sides give the fish a definite prehistoric look. In spite of its gnarly appearance, the white sturgeon is prized as a game fish as well as for its firm, white meat. Its eggs also make for some rib-stickin' caviar. Fishing for them in Montana, though, has been prohibited since 1979. Their numbers have been in steady decline, and efforts are currently under way to find ways to increase their spawning.

Like some mothers-in-law and members of Congress, the white sturgeon can live to be over one hundred years old. In the Kootenai River below the falls, where they congregate, you can just imagine one of the more geriatric specimens yelling at the younger sturgeon, "Hey, you kids, get off my spawning bed!"

Not only are they the oldest, but they're also among the biggest of landlocked game fish. Elsewhere in the U.S. sturgeon populations are healthy enough to allow for fishing. The world record is a 468-pounder, caught in 1983 in California. The biggest one ever captured was a 1,387-pound monster netted in the Fraser River, British Columbia, in 1897. It must have been quite a sight, seeing a dozen Canadian fishermen wetting their pants in unison.

Construction of the Libby Dam upstream pretty much doomed this particular population, and the resulting manipulation of river water levels has basically stopped any significant natural reproduction. At current attrition rates of 9 percent per year, it's estimated that the white sturgeon in the 30-mile stretch below the Kootenai Falls will be functionally extinct by 2065, unless new techniques and a resurgence in spawning somehow come into play.

It's too bad, because the unique sturgeon, although it's ugly enough to make a train take a dirt road, offers a glimpse into the prehistoric past of Montana's aquatic life. If you spend any time fishing for trout on the Kootenai, maybe you'll be lucky enough to see one of these rare fish. Just don't scream. You'll hurt its feelings.

The Kootenai Falls Trail System is located on the Kootenai River near milepost 21, between Troy and Libby on US 2.

Careful, Or They Might Roll Out Your Barrel
Lolo

Accordion players have suffered the poor jokes directed at their instrument for years. Example: What's the definition of perfect pitch? That's when you toss an accordion in the dumpster and it lands on a banjo.

But as any aficionado will tell you, the accordion is a versatile, complex instrument that, in the right hands, can make some of the best music you're likely to hear. In western Montana a couple hundred accordion players and fans gather every other week to drink, dance, chat, and mostly take turns entertaining each other with the squeezebox.

The Five Valley Accordion Association was founded in 1987 by Ruth and Les Gilfillan, two accomplished accordionists looking for like-minded musicians who enjoyed playing and hearing the instrument. From those humble beginnings of barely a dozen people, the association has grown over the years to around 200 members. They gather every other week, usually on Sunday afternoons, for jam

"Hey, do you guys know 'Inna Gadda Da Vida?'"

sessions. The session is in a different location each fortnight, scattered in different places in the Bitterroot and Missoula Valleys.

The camaraderie and shared love of music is evident at these gatherings. The dance floor is full all afternoon with waltzers, two-steppers, and other practitioners of the easygoing steps that require a big space and a shaker of dance floor powder.

There's always a rhythm section of drums and bass to accompany the accordions, and a wide variety of musicians always show up to share their talent and complement the squeezebox tones. Guitars, banjos, harmonicas, even singers appear on the stage for two or three songs at a time. Members crowd around the long banquet tables, drinking light beer or coffee, eating snacks out of Tupperware containers, and sharing gossip and news among friends. It's quite the social scene, and it's obvious everyone is enjoying the lively, constant stream of accordions.

The association has a sister group in Kalispell, with an even larger membership. The two groups gather for a big picnic each summer, and the Five Valleys group also has a scholarship program, awarding cash to promising young players.

Local newspapers usually list the time and location of upcoming jam sessions, and the members welcome any and all accordion players or fans of the instrument. Just leave your accordion jokes at home. They've heard 'em all.

For more information, call (406) 273-0722.

Nothing Like a Cold Beer on a Hot Girl
Lolo

There she sits, the buxom cowgirl wearing nothing but boots and hat, splashing happily in a giant mug of beer. She's oblivious to the passing traffic, paying no mind to the schoolchildren walking by. She would, but she's wood.

Perched atop the porch roof at KT's Hayloft Saloon in Lolo is a near life-size sculpture of an anatomically correct temptress cavorting in a mug of foamy brew. With one boot-clad leg raised up over her head, she seems to be having the time of her life.

The beer mug girl, which is also featured in the bar's logo, was carved in the 1970s by a Lincoln artist known as the Lost Woodsman. It's a graceful, exuberant sculpture that has become a Lolo landmark. At one point the bar's owners painted a brassiere on the Hayloft hottie to shield her ample breasts from the tender eyeballs of kids as they were walking to Lolo Elementary a couple of blocks away. But the paint has long since worn away, once again revealing an impressive pair of twin peaks standing firmly in the mountain sun.

The Hayloft also had a contest a few years back to find a woman who most closely resembled the beer mug girl. No word on who the winner was, but the idea of real live women plunging nude into a monster mug of cold beer is making me a little thirsty.

KI's Hayloft Saloon is located in Lolo, at 11885 US 93 South. Call (406) 273-2860 to ask what's on tap.

"Yes, your Honor, I do believe the naked girl in the giant beer mug had been drinking . . . "

The Super 8 Must Have Been Booked Up

Lolo

Lewis and Clark's journey to the Pacific and back is well documented, but precious little physical evidence was left by the explorers and their team. It might be the earliest known example of the "pack it in, pack it out" approach to camping.

But in Lolo, at the crossroads where US 12 from Idaho meets US 93, a few items have been discovered that support the Corps' journal reports that they did indeed spend several days, in 1805 and 1806, in the meadow near Lolo Creek that has come to be known as Travelers' Rest.

As with most of Lewis and Clark's discoveries along the expedition, the natives had beaten them to it. In fact, the whole area from the base of the Bitterroot Mountains clear up to Mormon Creek was considered a campground by the Nez Perce, Pend d'Oreille, and Salish tribes. Hunters, traders, and their families had congregated in the Travelers' Rest area for thousands of years to enjoy the plentiful game, the abundant edible and medicinal plants, and for the sanctuary and friendship shared among the tribes.

In 2002 archeologists discovered a metal military uniform button, a blue, glass trade bead, and a puddle of once-melted lead in what would have been a campsite for the Lewis and Clark Expedition's

Trivia

The country's first luge run was built in Lolo Hot Springs in 1965. It was closed down when two lost, inebriated men were discovered at the top of the run, trying to pee toward three oceans from one spot.

soldiers. This rare, tangible proof of the Corps of Discovery's presence immediately boosted the importance of the site, and it was made into a state park.

Thousands of school kids from nearby towns converge on the park each spring, and there are activities year-round. A well-groomed walking trail takes you across a sturdy bridge spanning Lolo Creek to the actual campsite area of the expedition members. Interpretive signs and an informative brochure point out significant areas and features of the trail.

There's a nominal fee to enter the park, but it's free for Montana residents. The Travelers' Rest area still carries a deep spiritual significance to Montana's Native American community, and it's definitely worth a visit to learn more about their culture and history. With any luck you'll be there when a tribal member is on-site, and he or she will be able to answer your questions firsthand.

To put your feet up in Travelers' Rest State Park, go to 10565 US 12 in Lolo. Open year-round, the hours are limited in the winter. Call (406) 273-4848 or explore your way to www.travelersrest.org.

Killer Kayaking Kreates Kurious Krowds
Missoula

Whitewater sprays into the air as they maneuver across the wave; they roll, they slide, they pull off glide turns, they bob to and fro like a child's walnut-shell ship in a gutter. Kayakers in their brightly colored craft travel from all over the world to swarm Brennan's Wave in Missoula, putting on a show for all comers at the very heart of town.

This man-made, carefully engineered, whitewater play pool in the Clark Fork River is named for Missoulian Brennan Guth, the world-class kayaker who died in 2001 at age thirty-two. Brennan's Wave was completed in 2006, and at most water levels it will allow for surfing, spinning, cartwheels, loops, helixes, and pretty much any other maneuvers the boaters can come up with.

At a cost of $325,000, the project is the result of an ambitious

★ ★

collaboration between the Missoula Whitewater Association, the World Class Kayak Academy, and the Missoula Redevelopment Agency, which recognized the need to remove the dangerous and unsightly water hazards from Missoula's downtown. The agency provided funds for the project, which was also underwritten by Modern Machinery, Envirocon, and the Dennis and Phyllis Washington Foundation.

Far more complex than simply dumping riprap into the river, the design and construction took five years and thousands of hours donated by the many supporters, friends, and relatives of Guth, a kayaking legend. A stone marker with Guth's likeness and the story of Brennan's Wave stands in Caras Park overlooking the wave.

There are three features to Brennan's Wave on the Clark Fork, and they occur at different water levels. It was designed so that the first and best-known feature comes in at a water flow volume of about 14,000 cubic feet per second. Once the flow drops to 11,000 cfs, it sustains front surfing only. The second feature is always visible, but really kicks in at about 10,000 cfs. The third feature reveals itself at the peak of the river flow, which occurs during spring runoff.

Spectators regularly gather at Caras Park, where an overlook gives them a bird's-eye view of paddlers in the wave, less than 30 yards away.

Kayakers can park right at Caras Park and enjoy this free play wave any time, except during particularly frigid winters when most of the river is covered in ice. Then again, that might be the best time for the chicken-hearted novice to give it a go.

Brennan's Wave is in the Clark Fork River at the edge of Caras Park, near Higgins Street.

May Be Suitable for Astronaut Training
Missoula

As you place one boot in the stirrup and swing yourself up into the saddle, you can feel the hum of energy coming from the beast beneath you. She wants to run. You tighten the leather strap around your waist, wrap your hands around the chrome pole, and suddenly the horse begins to move. "Hold on tight, riders!" yells the operator over the loudspeaker.

A Carousel for Missoula is under way.

One of the fastest carousels in the country, this contraption whips around at nearly 8 miles per hour on the outside row of ponies. It may not sound like much, but the centrifugal force generated at that speed requires a tight grip on the pole, and you've got to firmly clench that hand-carved horse between your thighs to avoid getting hurled off your mount, which would surely be videotaped by someone, and you'd wind up on YouTube before you got back to the hotel.

The brainchild of Missoula cabinet maker Chuck Kaparich, the carousel is an immensely popular feature of the Garden City. Kaparich spent many hours of his childhood riding the carousel at Columbia Gardens in Butte (which closed in 1973), and had already purchased an antique carousel frame and carved four horses when he proposed the project to the Missoula City Council in 1991. By the time it opened in 1995, a huge team of carvers, mechanics, and other volunteers had worked for over 100,000 hours to create this beautiful, incredibly detailed work of art that operates year-round in its circus tent–shaped enclosure by the Clark Fork River.

Thousands of people ride the carousel each year, whooping and laughing along with the music that flows out of the largest operating band organ in the U.S. Trombones, saxophones, xylophones, and several percussion instruments are driven by more than 400 hand-made wooden pipes. Even the organ's façade is a hand-carved work of art, depicting a cliff-top castle under siege by dragons, flanked by knights on charging stallions.

Volunteers work continuously to keep the carousel in tip-top shape, a comforting thought when you're careening around atop one of the outer horses, hanging on for dear life and hoping not to refund your Slurpee.

★ ★

A Carousel for Missoula is located in Caras Park, at 101 Carousel Drive. They're open year-round, and can be reached by calling (406) 549-8382.

It's a Good Thing Missoula Has Two Hospitals
Missoula

"I'm learning to fly, but I ain't got wings. Coming down is the hardest thing." Tom Petty probably wasn't thinking about gelande ski jumpers when he wrote that lyric, but he may as well have been. He could have called the song "Crazy Fools With a Death Wish."

An annual rite of spring, the gelande competition in Missoula is one of only three gelandes currently held in the U.S. Skiers jump for distance and style points, and try not to get busted up in the process. Gelande differs from regular, Olympic-style ski jumping in that the skiers here use regular alpine skis and fixed-heel bindings. They wear Lycra racing suits and jump with poles. The skis themselves are longish at 220 centimeters, but other than that, any of these maniacs could be just another downhiller next to you on the chairlift.

Hundreds of ski jump fans and Bloody Mary enthusiasts gather at the bottom of the forty-five-degree jump hill, which is the width of a two-lane road and situated in a narrow chute between two rocky knolls. Skiers propel themselves up off the flat launch table at 55 miles per hour and fly across 80 feet of flat terrain before it drops off into the landing track. They try to hold the classic V posture with their skis as they fly 200 feet and beyond before slapping down to earth, then zooming directly under a lift line full of cheering skiers, making an immediate hard left turn to avoid crashing into the orange storm fence and/or hurtling off the mountain into a canyon.

"Once you jump farther than 160 feet, you're basically just falling out of the sky," observed one gelande veteran, who still seemed to have a couple of his marbles. Evidence of the crazy nature of this event is all around. Some skiers display their cabin fever by wearing Halloween masks as they schuss down the slope, and cold beer flows

★ ★

freely, especially if it's a bluebird spring day on the mountain.

Sunshine and mild temperatures are especially welcomed by the jumper who wins the amateur class, because Missoula's gelande tradition calls for this high-flying fellow to make the final jump of the day wearing nothing but skis, boots, and a big smile.

For more information, talk to Snowbowl Ski and Summer Resort at (406) 549-9777. They also have a Web address: www.montanasnow bowl.com.

**This takes a lot more cojones than riding
a barstool down the street.**

★ ★

There's Gnome Place Like Home
Missoula

When a Keebler elf bakes his final cookie and goes to his great reward, he might hope to wind up at the Gnome House in the Missoula Public Library.

This twenty-three room, six-story house was built over a ten-year period by Missoula's Mona Frangos. It stands nearly 6 feet tall in its wood and glass display case. Constructed in a hollow log, the Gnome House is overflowing with hundreds upon hundreds of pieces of elfin furniture, decorations, and the detritus of daily, uh, gnome life.

A miniature copy of the *New York Times* sits on the kitchen table. It's smaller than a matchbook, but can actually be read with a magnifying glass. Sample headline: "Obsessed Giant Crafts Gnome Home, Leprechauns Demand Low-Income Housing."

Mona's fascination with elves and gnomes began in her childhood, and she spent her formative years building miniature houses in hollow stumps in the woods. She furnished these houses with bits and pieces she would gather on her walks, and later supplemented them with antique doll furniture from an aunt. Some of this furniture is over one hundred years old, and now helps fill out the Gnome House in Missoula's library.

Strings of tiny lights wind between floors in the Gnome House, illuminating a vibrant, lived-in space that gives the impression that the inhabitants have just stepped out. The top floor contains a fully outfitted artist's studio, complete with an unfinished oil painting propped on an easel. Below the studio is a cozy, book-lined study that looks like a good place for big decisions to be made, like which curly-toed shoes to wear today, or perhaps whether to fly or walk to work.

You can't miss it when you enter the library; it's just inside the front doors upstairs. Gnomes, fairies, elves, and other fantasy creatures would give their left wing to live in this world-class miniature

★ ★

**If this isn't a clear argument for legalizing
weed, I don't know what is.**

home. The amount of detail is mind-boggling, and you can literally spend hours studying all the whimsical items filling the woodsy
house. If you're in Missoula, take the time to check it out. It's uncom-
monly good.

The Missoula Public Library is located at 301 East Main Street, Missoula. They're open for a little browsing Monday through Thursday,
from 10 a.m. to 9 p.m., on Friday and Saturday from 10 a.m. to 6
p.m., and on Sunday from 1 to 5 p.m.

Paul Harvey: It All Started in Missoula

"This is Paul Harvey. Stand by for *news.*"

So began the late broadcaster Paul Harvey's *News and Comment* on the ABC Radio Networks, which beamed his daily radio show to some 25 million listeners on 1,200 radio stations around the world. But not too many people know that America's most beloved radio broadcaster began his career in a stuffy little studio in Missoula, Montana.

KGVO Radio boss A. J. "Art" Mosby hired Paul Harvey Aurandt, a newlywed, twenty-two-year-old greenhorn from Tulsa, to do man-on-the-street interviews along North Higgins. Harvey soon indulged in some theater of the mind, telling listeners that he was flying around in a plane visiting small towns in the area, when he was actually broadcasting from the tiny studio above the Top Hat bar in downtown Missoula. His delivery was convincing enough that people began going outside to scan the skies for his aircraft, or would call the station to see when he'd be flying over.

Harvey's starting salary of $29 a week was a humble beginning, especially compared to the $100 million contract he signed with ABC Radio Networks in 2000. Before his death in 2009, Harvey shared his fond memories of his year in Missoula in a taped birthday greeting to Mosby.

"Remember the time I threw the union organizer down the stairs and almost got you in a peck of legal trouble?" Harvey laughed. He also reminded Mosby of Harvey's first football broadcast, expressing his appreciation for his boss's patience: "Anybody but you would have chased me out of Missoula and out of the industry after that disastrous bluff."

Paul Harvey's first studio isn't exactly Abbey Road.

Mosby eventually did fire Harvey, telling him that he had a silly-sounding delivery and should forget about broadcasting and go into advertising. But, of course, after Harvey left Missoula for Chicago, his career began its meteoric rise, and he quickly became one of the most popular and beloved radio broadcasters in history. And to think it all began in that dusty little studio over the Top Hat.

And now you know the rest of the story.

The Top Hat is located at 134 West Front Street in Missoula.

★ ★

This Bus Is a Cat's Worst Nightmare
Missoula

Driving around Missoula, you might spy a short bus full of passengers, but this one differs from the official school variety in some important ways. First, it's not yellow but rather a bright-orange or lime-green shade that's impossible to miss. Second, and more importantly, the passengers are all dogs.

The bus (there are two of them, actually) belongs to GoFetch!, an upscale dog supply store with three locations in Missoula. The busload of dogs is either on its way to, or coming home from, an off-leash mountain hike up Pattee Canyon. Five days a week, GoFetch! employees make the rounds in their buses, picking up dogs from their homes to take them on an 8-mile, three-hour hike in the backcountry.

"Does this bus go downtown?" "Very funny. Just get in."

"Dogs have an innate tendency to be a part of a pack. It's a joy-ful thing to witness," says GoFetch! owner Scott Timothy, who runs packs up the mountainside two days a week himself. "Those are my therapy days," he says with a laugh.

Indeed, it's the pack mentality that allows the off-leash exercise program to work so well. Dogs are pre-screened, and aggressive animals are not accepted for the program. The animals won't run away, says Timothy, because they like to be with the other dogs. Fights are rare, even among these large packs (twelve to fifteen dogs) of various breeds.

"Some dogs are too shy at first, but I have seen dogs become more outgoing and more sociable after spending time in the pack," says Timothy. He adds that they start the timid dogs on a leash, and gradually work them into the pack.

But it's not doggie boot camp, by any means. "We're facilitators of fun. We're not drill sergeants. When you're working with dogs, you can be playful and still garner respect from your pack."

Like Jane Goodall and her chimps, Timothy immerses himself in the pack, and is treated by the dogs as the alpha male. That ability to walk on his hind legs must be mighty impressive to his canine crew.

For more information, call (406) 728-BARK or visit www.gofetch dog.com.

If Only We Could Get That Ghost to Mow the Yard
Missoula

Built around 1900, the lovely Victorian dwelling at 319 South Fifth West in Missoula began as the showplace home of a University of Montana professor. But after several mishaps and untimely deaths throughout its history, the stately abode on this quiet, tree-lined residential street has become known as the "House of Screams."

It started in the 1940s when Eleanor Zakos, the wife of Jim's Café owner Jim Zakos, heard a spine-chilling scream that seemingly emanated from the walls. Her sister was also in the house, and they both agreed that there were two screams, starting low and then building to a high shriek. Police, firemen, electricians, plumbers—no one could find a logical source of the screams, which continued at all hours of the night and day, never predictably.

A family friend, Reverend Andrew Landin, offered to perform an exorcism on the building after Mrs. Zakos's brother-in-law, John Lambros, passed away in 1956. The entire surviving family held hands and slowly moved from room to room, while Reverend Landin prayed for the malevolent spirit to skedaddle. A family friend who was also present at the exorcism later said, "Us kids had the living crap scared out of us." There were no reports of anyone's head spinning around or vomiting pea soup. Not that kind of exorcism, I guess.

The effort was successful, evidently, because the screams stopped. The stories, however, continued through the years, becoming more lurid and graphic as they were retold. The house was abandoned for years and fell into disrepair, until the neighbors tried to have the old eyesore demolished. Missoula contractor Mark Estep decided to buy the house, however, and the Victorian home has been restored to its original beauty. It stands today as a testament to the tortured lives it once held, and while no screams have been heard for years, many locals remain convinced that the tormented souls of the home's previous inhabitants haunt its rooms, trying to break through from the other side.

Or maybe it's just a neighborhood cat.

The House of Screams is a private residence located at 319 South Fifth West in Missoula.

Here's the Skinny on Montana's Iwo Jima Connection
Missoula

Tucked away on the sprawling expanse of Fort Missoula, there's a neat little collection of military items that holds a unique place in the history of Montana's involvement in WWII.

The Rocky Mountain Museum of Military History is a pair of

★ ★

smallish buildings housing two rooms of military equipment, models, photos, uniforms, and stories. The buildings are easy enough to find—there's a Vietnam-era Iroquois helicopter parked next to them.

The Vietnam War is well represented within the museum, but the most impressive display concerns Missoula's most noted soldier, PFC Louis C. Charlo. A great-grandson of Salish Chief Charlo, Louis was one of a half-dozen marines who raised the first U.S. flag atop Mount Suribachi on Iwo Jima. The story of the flag raisings (a second, larger flag was raised, which is the one in the famous photo by Joe Rosenthal) is well documented, and the centerpiece of the display is a highly detailed, 4-foot-long replica of the USS *Missoula,* the attack transport that delivered the soldiers to the beach for one of WWII's bloodiest battles.

Other military vehicles are represented by dozens of meticulously constructed, period-correct models. There's even a full-size replica of a horse, complete with saddle and feedbag.

Mannequins are arranged in the museum, displaying various American military garb throughout the history of our country, dating back to the Revolutionary War. Individual Montana soldiers killed in action are memorialized through several displays featuring their photos, stories, and memorabilia.

There's even a nod to the ladies, with informational displays honoring nurses, officers' wives, and Cathy Williams, the buffalo soldier. Many of the wartime posters feature WAC recruiting pitches and Rosie the Riveter–style exhortations for civilians to continue their sacrifice for the war effort.

In one display from the Iraq conflict, a small slip of paper has the story of a soldier being interviewed by the media. The report asks the soldier, a marine, if he can ever forgive Osama Bin Laden. The soldier's answer: "It's God's responsibility to forgive Bin Laden. It's the responsibility of the United States Marine Corps to arrange the meeting."

The Rocky Mountain Museum of Military History is open from 12 to 5 p.m. seven days a week during the summer, and on weekends only between Labor Day and June 1. It is located in buildings T-310 and T-316 at Fort Missoula. Call (406) 549-5346 for more information, or visit www.fortmissoula.org.

Hey, You Got Your Museum All Over My Store
Missoula

Just west of Missoula, out past the airport on MT 10, lies a mind-boggling treasure trove of Americana. It's the Montana Museum of Work History, located within the Axmen store. Known ostensibly for selling wood stoves, the Axmen's owners, Guy and Grant Hanson, are lifelong collectors who have an eye for the unusual, but also for the more common-but-interesting items of everyday American life.

One of the earliest acquisitions on display is a 1919 Pierce Arrow truck, which was acquired from a farmer by a young Grant Hanson in 1963, who swapped his mother's golf clubs for the rundown wreck. His mother was less than pleased, of course, but presumably calmed down when they learned that the vehicle was ultra-rare, one of only four left in the U.S.

The museum celebrates "ordinary Montanans who did extraordinary things," according to the museum's book of stories and recipes. Displays include antique firearms, vintage military gear, vehicles, tools of all description, toys, sporting equipment, and an endless variety of things that Montanans have used to survive the sometimes harsh climate.

You'll see soy license plates, which were produced during WWII when metal was scarce due to the war effort. The soy plates are extremely rare, however, because many of them were eaten right off the vehicles by livestock, who found them quite tasty.

Up the stairs, past the overhead tracks supporting a scale replica of a Shay gear drive locomotive, there's a corner containing dozens of antique outboard motors flanking an artfully displayed collection of vintage fishing lures. Across the room, there's a boat up on the

It's just like your grandpa's garage. If he
was a demented pack rat.

wall, mounted to appear as if it's actually crashing through the corner of the building.

Other walls contain varieties of tools, including planes, plus logging
equipment, camping gear, and all kinds of farming machinery.

They'll give you a tour at the drop of a hat, and you'll find yourself
lost in the mists of Montana history, taking in all the tools and equipment used through the past to carve out a life in this rugged state.
Just make sure you lock your golf clubs in the trunk; you never know
about those Hanson boys.

The Axmen is located at 7655 West MT 10 in Missoula. Call (406)
728-7020 to ask about tours.

Just Don't Call Them Toadstools

Montana has its share of mushroom enthusiasts, to be sure. There are even quite a few who would be considered mycological experts. But how many have starred in an award-winning mushroom documentary?

Exactly one. Larry Evans, the "Indiana Jones of Mushrooms," is easy to spot at Missoula's Farmer's Market—he's the one with the 2-foot-tall red-and-white-striped top hat, the shoulder-length silver braids, and the mischievous twinkle in his shiitake-colored eyes. *Know Your Mushrooms,* a feature-length documentary featuring Larry, by Canadian filmmaker Ron Mann, was released in 2009. "It's an animated garden of delight," says the Mushroom Man with a sly grin.

Larry has also written and recorded two CDs packed with songs about mushrooms, many of them sung in his craggy baritone. Top musicians from western Montana were involved in both projects, most notably Zoe Wood, who sang "Naemaetaloma" on the *Today Show.*

Since identifying his first edible mushroom, a Slippery Jack, at the age of ten, Larry has been immersed in the world of mycology. He's traveled the world educating people about hunting, identifying, cultivating, and using mushrooms. Everywhere he goes, he says, he soaks up the local culture and knowledge about mushrooms.

"I left a mushroom as a tip in a Chinese restaurant once," he says, explaining how the Chinese revere the fungus for its spiritual and medicinal powers. "They were jazzed!"

There is a lot we can learn about mushrooms from other cultures, says the fungal guru. While largely relegated to the level of a mere garnish or side dish in the U.S., the lowly 'shroom is a major source of protein, he says, and can be an integral part of solving the nutritional challenges facing many parts of the world. "The Russians get it. They eat mushrooms we consider inedible, because they know how to process them properly."

Aside from its value as a food source, the mushroom is also widely used for its medicinal properties. Over 500 varieties of mushroom are traded worldwide for use as pharmaceutical tools.

Another side to the mushroom that gets a lot of play is the psychedelic aspect. Larry has his own theories about the cultural significance and history of the "Magic Mushroom." The *Amanita muscaria*, with its bright red and white cap, has been used for its hallucinogenic properties for centuries. "Why do you think Santa Claus is dressed in red and white?" Larry asks, adjusting his own red-and-white top hat. "And how do you think he got those reindeer to fly?"

For more poop about mushrooms, drift over to the Western Montana Mycological Association's Web site: www.fungaljungal.org.

"You should invite me to your party— I'm a fungi!"

★ ★

Montana's Most Interesting Store

Missoula

So you've got a wild evening planned, and you need to buy some organic bubble bath, a Rammstein CD, a sympathy card, and a rubber chicken? Well, there's a store in Missoula where you can find all that, and a whole lot more.

Rockin' Rudy's is a vast, one-of-a-kind retail establishment that's more of an experience than a store. For many Montanans who visit Missoula, Rudy's is a must-stop where they can let their retail freak flag fly. What started out as a modest record store in 1982 has transformed and grown over the years into a sprawling, intensely eclectic monument to fun, currently housed in an old Eddy's Bakery just south of the Clark Fork River.

Bruce Miklus, the ponytailed founder and driving force behind Rockin' Rudy's, has an uncanny knack for stocking and selling a wide variety of interesting items that keep people coming back, providing new surprises every time they come through his door.

Rudy's (from Miklus's boyhood nickname, Rudolph) is a riot of color, bursting with a wild assortment of greeting cards, toys and novelties, body products, incense and candles, handcrafted jewelry, top-drawer chocolate, and of course, music. The cavernous store is punctuated with displays featuring Bruce's favorite musician and inspiration, Elvis Presley. You'll see several life-size statues and cardboard cutouts of the King, as well as his gold records and other rock 'n roll paraphernalia. But that's the *only* paraphernalia you'll see.

"We never sold that head shop stuff," Bruce says. "We consciously decided that's not where we want to go." Consequently, people of all ages, lifestyles, and tax brackets are comfortable browsing their way through the store, checking out the risqué greeting cards, hand-carved Buddha statues, and practical jokes.

"Music is still the backbone of our business," says Bruce, but he has positioned the store in such a way that Rudy's is hardly affected by the ongoing demise of the brick-and-mortar record store. "It's a smaller slice of the pie. I used to be concerned about a Tower Records or something coming into Missoula, but the whole paradigm of retailing music has changed. And so have we."

Indeed, when Rudy's was located in a small storefront just a few blocks north of their current location, vinyl record albums took up most of the floor space. Bruce gradually expanded his line to include greeting cards and gifts, and now you can find just about anything your heart desires in Rockin' Rudy's, whether your wild night requires a feather boa, a string of cowboy boot lights, or a boxing Jesus hand puppet.

Not too many books, though, Bruce adds. "If you want to sell books, you have to be a book store."

Deep thoughts, from the kingpin of Montana's most interesting store.

Rockin' Rudy's can be found at 237 Blaine Street, and reached at (406) 542-0077 or www.rockinrudys.com.

Do You Believe in Ghosts?
Missoula

The University Theatre, on the campus of the University of Montana in Missoula, has hosted hundreds of world-class events in it eighty-plus years of existence, many of which have been enjoyed by a capacity crowd of 1,140 people. Well, make that 1,141 if you include the ghost.

In 1996 a crew member was helping to install rigging above the proscenium stage when the scaffolding suddenly collapsed, sending the man plummeting 60 feet to his death. The tragedy cast a pall on the theater, and deeply affected those who were present. But more theater workers would be touched by the accident in the coming years.

"I was sitting up in the light box, and the ghost light on the stage was on," says Shy Obrigewitch, the University Theatre's assistant technical director. "I looked down, and on the left side of the stage, something appeared. It didn't have any legs from the knees down. It walked about 25 feet and then disappeared." Was it the spirit of the scaffolding accident victim? Obrigewitch declined to speculate, but he is quite sure of what he saw.

Other deaths have occurred in the theater over the years, and the building has long been rumored to be haunted by the ghosts of these unfortunate souls. A professor reportedly committed suicide in the 1950s, and some years ago a student fell into a stage well and died.

Tom Webster, the theater director, has felt a presence in the offices at times, and believes that the building is haunted. "I get the heebie jeebies," he says. "It's a grand old building, and it has a lot of soul. But you know it's just got to have some paranormal activity, because of the history."

So if you happen to see a play or a concert at the University Theatre, just know that somewhere in the balcony, up in the rigging, or maybe even in the (supposedly) empty seat next to you, the University Theatre ghost may be enjoying the show as well.

The University Theatre is located on the campus of the University of Montana.

Wild Animals Marching Downtown
Missoula

On a Saturday in mid-May each spring, the streets of downtown Missoula come alive with wildlife. Sharp-eyed observers can witness dozens of species moving casually along Main Street. Hippos rumble along next to cheetahs, snakes share the path with owls and hawks. Wolves amble along, seemingly oblivious to their erstwhile prey in the procession. They also seem to ignore the wagons and baby strollers carrying bats, coyotes, and the occasional baby elephant.

Welcome to Missoula's Wild Walk Parade, which kicks off the annual International Wildlife Film Festival. Kids of all ages—but mostly under ten—spend weeks getting ready for the Wild Walk, constructing elaborate costumes of their favorite critters. Or sometimes they just paint antlers on a big piece of cardboard.

You don't see this often in nature: a leopard
with crocs on his feet.

★ ★

Each year's parade has a theme that is loosely followed by the participants. Some recent themes have been "Creatures of the Night," "Howling at the Moon," and "Don't Put That In Your Mouth." Okay, I made up the last one, but the various themes help guide the creativity of the different schools and daycare groups that enter their kids in the parade.

The procession moves along Main Street for a couple of blocks, then winds its way down to Caras Park for the Wild Fest, which provides an afternoon of fun activities for the wee ones, including a "costume show," where they get to walk across a stage and receive applause for their outfits.

Some parents really get into the act, either donning their own animal costumes or incorporating themselves into their children's schemes. Other parents are in the parade purely to provide locomotion. After a couple of blocks, many of the smaller creatures run out of steam, and are hefted onto parental shoulders for the remainder of the route.

The International Wildlife Film Festival is a world-renowned event that draws visitors and exhibitors to Missoula from all over the world. For more than thirty years, the festival has hosted the absolute finest cinematic efforts in the wildlife film world. But to a four-year-old leopard, snoozing in a carrier on his daddy's back, none of that matters. The excitement and the glory of the Wild Walk Parade is an end in itself.

The International Wildlife Media Center and Film Festival offices are located at 718 South Higgins Avenue in Missoula. Call (406) 728-9380 for information, or take a stroll past www.wildlifefilms.org.

They Kept Bears in There
Missoula

When the Greenough family of Missoula donated twenty acres of prime streamside land across from their mansion for a city park in 1902, they gave explicit instructions that the land be maintained in its

It certainly looks like it could hold a bear. Or maybe a teenager.

pristine, natural state. Sure thing, said the city officials. But what the city needed was a zoo.

So a small zoo was built, including the only part that still stands, an octagonal-shaped bear cage made from limestone hauled up from Rattlesnake Creek.

No one knows who actually built the bear cage, but they probably had no trouble keeping it full. The Rattlesnake Wilderness is prime black bear habitat, and the pesky bruins frequently make their way into the lower Rattlesnake neighborhoods to raid trash cans, scarf dog food, and generally make themselves a pain in the butt. The

★ ★

cage is no longer used, of course, and in recent years has fallen into disrepair due to erosion and vandalism.

In the summer of 2009, Philip Maechling, Missoula's historic preservation officer, spearheaded an effort to restore and repair the crumbling cage. Maechling hoped that, in the process, the story of the bear cage would emerge. Several longtime Missoula residents shared their memories of going down to Greenough Park to peer through the cage bars at the bear inside. Some recall doing so as recently as the 1940s.

The bear cage sits dug partially into the hillside, right on the black-top park path about 100 yards from the south entrance. You can look into the dim interior and see the individual dens that were excavated for the bears. The walls are nearly 2 feet thick, and the roof overhead is lined with steel railroad rails. It's an odd little structure, a one-hundred-year-old reminder of the clueless approach to preserving wildlife that was employed by Missoula at the turn of the last century.

The Greenough Park bear cage is right next to the walk/bike path, about 100 yards north of the southern entrance to the park.

You Should Have Been Here for the Bison-tennial . . .

Moiese

The deer and the antelope play throughout Montana, but on the picturesque Palouse prairie near Moiese, you'll find a home where the buffalo roam. Well, technically, they're bison, but the term "buffalo" has been used for the American bison for so long that the two terms have become interchangeable. Kind of like "reality TV" and "toxic landfill."

The National Bison Range, established in 1908, was the nation's first wildlife refuge, created to help save these magnificent animals from extinction. In the mid-1800s some 70 million bison thundered across the plains of the American West. But decades of indiscriminate hunting and slaughter by white settlers and pioneers nearly

★ ★

"What are you lookin' at?"

eradicated the species, until fewer than one hundred animals
remained in the wild. Several hundred bison had been captured and
bred, however, and the populations slowly grew back to the point
where they are now no longer in danger of extinction.

Today there are anywhere between 350 and 500 bison roaming
around the 18,500-acre Bison Range, which is a part of the National
Wildlife Refuge System. Miles of gravel roads wind through the
grasslands, forest, and wetlands of the Bison Range, and you'll get
up close and personal with dozens of species of wildlife, birds, and
plants.

★ ★

You won't find a more powerful symbol of the Wild West than these large, menacing beasts. The males typically weigh a ton, and they're usually in a foul mood. Females are about half that weight, but can be just as nasty if they sense a threat to their calves.

On a recent trip to photograph some bison for this book, I was standing on the road about 50 feet from my car, snapping photos of a small group of large males who were rolling in the dirt to cool off. A park ranger came walking by and told me I'd have to get closer to my vehicle. "Like 5 feet away," he said ominously. I pointed out that he was on foot with no protection, and asked him what he would do if a bison charged. No way could he outrun a bison.

"Oh, I don't have to outrun the bison," he said with a smile. "I only have to outrun you."

The National Bison Range is located at 132 Bison Range Road in Moiese. There is a large visitor's center with displays and information. Their phone number is (406) 644-2211.

Black With a White Stripe, Or White With Black Stripes?
Paradise

If you find yourself driving along MT 200 northwest of Paradise, there's a good chance you're going to see some pretty weird-looking cows. Think zebras. Think penguins. Think pandas.

Sure, there are other breeds of black-and-white cows, but these babies are striking. The herd, owned by a local rancher, are all black with a big white band around the middle. Or are they white with a big black band at each end? I guess it's kind of a chicken-or-the-egg thing.

The breed, known as the Dutch belted, dates back to the seventeenth century when it was known as Lakenvelder. Evidently, the idea was for nobility to breed animals of all different colors, but mostly black with a white band around the middle. The Lakenvelders turned

⭐ ⭐

out to be pretty good milk producers, and yielded a very lean beef. The Dutch were pretty stingy with the breed, though, and fewer than 200 purebred Dutch belteds are listed in the U.S.

You'll see some of them for sure, though, as you drive along the Flathead River on MT 200 between Dixon and Paradise. Do not attempt to adjust your set. They're supposed to look like that.

This herd looks like it was attacked by a madman with a paint roller.

★ ★

Plains's Multi-Function Grainry
Plains

I asked Sherry McCartney of Plains what it took to convert a feed and grain silo into an eclectic art gallery.

The Man Who Puts the Effort in Joint Effort

Missoula's reputation as a hippie enclave is only partially deserved, as hippies make up just a small slice of the big psychedelic pie that is Montana's second-largest city. It's true that Missoula is home to lots of hippies, young and old, but the Garden City's progressive atmosphere also breeds lots of artists, poets, actors, musicians, writers, freaks, and weirdos. Sometimes all in one person.

Which brings us to Uncle Bill Stoianoff, a standout Missoula character since the hippie heyday of the late '60s. But these days, when he talks about twisting one up, he means sausage. He's been making his own brand of gourmet links since 1990, and sells them exclusively at the Clark Fork outdoor market in the summer, and in his own store, the Joint Effort, year-round. An irrepressible raconteur, Uncle Bill has more stories than an Italian sausage has fennel seeds, and if you're lucky enough to catch him working the counter at the Joint Effort, wearing his ever-present black beret and a devious twinkle in his eye, make sure you've got some time on your hands.

He'll blow your mind with tales of the Montana Legends Bikers, a "group of two-wheel enthusiasts of a non-conforming persuasion," while you browse his unique inventory of playthings, postcards,

★ ★

"About three months and a hundred gallons of bleach," she laughed. "It took that long to clean out the layers and layers of pigeon and mouse poop."

Once those pests and their leavings were cleared out, McCartney

cookbooks, DayGlo posters, tobacco accessories, and a nostalgia-sparking collection of classic metal wind-up toys.

And then there's the hot sauce. Uncle Bill's House of Hot Sauce is an institution unto itself, boasting dozens of exotic and wonderful condiments from around the world, many of which can bring tears to your eyes just by reading the label. Uncle Bill is a true foodie, having studied under world-renowned chef Paul Prudhomme in 1987, and his educated palate is reflected in the selection of hot sauce. "These sauces have flavor. They don't just show off with raw heat."

Still, Uncle Bill's Sausages remain closest to his heart. The local favorite, he says, is the French Morel, which contains the succulent but seasonal morel mushroom, Madeira wine, and some spices he declines to reveal. One of Missoula's most well-loved rascals, Uncle Bill will make sure your visit to the Joint Effort is one you won't soon forget.

When I last spoke with Bill, my twelve-year-old son made it a point to compliment him on his sausage. "I really love the sweet Italian," he said. "That's my favorite."

"Me too," said Uncle Bill with a wink. "Her name's Loretta."

Joint Effort is located at 1918 Brooks Street in the Holiday Village shopping center. Give them a call at (406) 543-5627.

★ ★

and a host of volunteers transformed the one-time feed and grain store into one of western Montana's most interesting collections of original art, handmade crafts, and second-hand treasures.

The seventeen vendors that make up the Grainry Gallery offer a mind-boggling variety of stuff, from antler art to vintage pocket watches to used paperbacks. One vendor offers handmade coin purses and handbags, which are on display near a case full of Native handcrafted jewelry. Mother Lode, another vendor, has some very upscale, unique items including a silver and turquoise necklace of real bear claws, with a price tag of $750.

Vendors come and go, says McCartney, but the number remains steady at seventeen. Her own contribution to the Grainry Gallery is her corner booth filled with Plains memorabilia. Having grown up here, Sherry has spent her life collecting high school yearbooks, newspaper clippings, letter sweaters, and all kinds of local historical items. Her collection is the closest thing that Plains has to a local historical museum.

It could take an entire afternoon to wend your way through the Grainry, soaking up all the local history and handcrafted art. The exterior of the building may look like it belongs on a farm, but the inside is chock full of interesting treasures for the curious traveler. Oh, and it's also the local chamber of commerce visitor's center.

The Grainry Gallery is located at 602 Central Avenue South in Plains. They're open seven days a week from 10 a.m. to 6 p.m., with shorter hours in winter. Call (406) 826-8400 to find out more.

It's Hard to Putt With a Dinosaur Breathing Down Your Neck
Plains

Kids love dinosaurs, and kids love go-karts. Kids also love miniature golf. Hey, that gives me an idea!

Too late—there's already such a combination of childhood faves on display at the Piccadilly Park Family Fun Center near Plains. It's right next to MT 200. Don't worry, you can't miss it. In fact, you

★ ★

The last person to get a hole in one here
was Fred Flintstone.

might just choke on your Corn Nuts as you drive by and see a snarling *Tyrannosaurus* suddenly looming up out of the lush foliage of the well-manicured putt-putt course.

He stands over 10 feet tall, this hospital room green replica of the most fearsome of all reptiles. He looks like he's thinking of his next meal as he gazes over his shoulder at a placid *Brontosaurus*, which stands guard over the third hole several yards away. A few giant, colorful fiberglass mushrooms also dot the mini golf landscape, just in case it's not quite surreal enough to see a couple of huge dinosaurs standing around the western Montana plains.

★ ★

Englishman Peter Saunders and his wife, Jody, bought the Fun Center in 2004, and with the help of their kids, transformed the run-down roadside attraction into a thriving, attractive oasis for families traveling the highway between Thompson Falls and Ravalli.

"It brings families together," says Saunders, "even teenagers who say, 'I'm too cool for this.' After eight minutes on the go-karts, they're slapping each other on the back and having a great time." He adds that he and his own family have had all kinds of fun running the place, watching tourists from every state, as well as Canada and South America, pull in for some summer high jinks.

The Fun Center also boasts a set of batting cages, and there's a shaded picnic area near the big tree with the tire swing. But it's those big old dinosaurs that keep drawing your eye, and just might give you enough of a shiver to blow your par putt on that tricky swinging-log hole.

The Piccadilly Park Family Fun Center is located at 19 Kruger Road on MT 200 near Plains. Call (406) 826-7422 to schedule your own Jurassic putt.

This Is What Happens When Your Spouse Can't Throw Anything Away
Polson

So you think New York City's MOMA is impressive? The Louvre has a few interesting pieces? Well, those places will look like a trailer-park yard sale once you've spent a day at the Miracle of America Museum in Polson.

This sprawling, wildly eclectic testament to American culture and history lies alongside US 93 North, at the south end of Flathead Lake. As you park outside the museum's entrance, you'll be welcomed by a colorful metal sculpture of "Flessie," the Flathead Lake Monster. Don't let the building's unassuming exterior fool you; the museum's appearance doesn't begin to hint at the sheer volume and variety of items contained within its walls.

★ ★

The museum houses a seemingly endless series of displays depicting life in America during different eras. There are looms and spinning wheels from the early 1800s, kitchen items and appliances from every decade of the twentieth century, and fascinating collections of everyday Americana, from egg beaters to children's tricycles. One case holds a shocking array of racially charged items from the mid-twentieth century, from an embroidered KKK hood to an autographed copy of Eldridge Cleaver's book, *Soul on Fire*. Just around

What, you thought we wouldn't have a
two-headed calf in this book?

the corner, society's more-enlightened side is represented with a fully restored 1914 Mill's Violano, sitting next to several antique Victrolas.

You want to see an antique motorcycle? There are more than a dozen. A sheep-powered treadmill? You bet. Women's dresses and hats from the 1890s to the 1950s? There's a department store's worth. A flying monkey from *The Wizard of Oz?* Here's a life-size replica. There are classic children's windup toys, a full display of Boy Scouts paraphernalia, and an entire drugstore soda fountain, complete with a classic jukebox and a stuck-up waitress (mannequin).

If you're a military buff, welcome to Valhalla. The museum is heavy on the military and war-era items, and you can examine hundreds of rifles and pistols, along with uniforms and regalia from all branches of the armed service. Their collection of wartime posters is unique and thought-provoking.

Outside, among the museum's thirty-five separate buildings, you'll find dozens of tractors, jeeps, tanks, boats, cars, amphibious vehicles, troop carriers, ambulances, sleighs, and even a few helicopters. And don't forget the Vietnam-era Corsair jet you can see from the highway.

If you go, make sure you have the better part of a day to take it all in. You might not see the *Mona Lisa,* but how many art lovers have the opportunity to gaze upon an authentic two-headed calf?

The Miracle of America Museum is at 36094 Memory Lane, just south of Polson along US 93. Call (406) 883-6804 or browse past www.miracleofamericamuseum.org.

Even Captain Kangaroo Would Have Been Creeped Out
Polson

Inside the Polson-Flathead Historical Museum is perhaps one of Montana's most bizarre historical tributes to the Lewis and Clark Expedition. It's a meticulously detailed, somewhat-creepy group of handcrafted marionettes, set around a campfire in a large display

"Okay, everyone, 'I'm Your Puppet'
in C. One, two, three, four . . ."

case. Capt. Meriwether Lewis, Capt. William Clark, Sacagawea, and several members of the expedition are represented by 2-foot-tall likenesses.

Puppeteer Blanche Harding built the marionettes, which, upon closer inspection, are really quite charming, functional works of art. She passed away in 2004, and left more than a dozen marionettes to the museum, including the Lewis and Clark bunch, which comprises most of the collection.

The 9,000-square-foot museum is bulging with hundreds of artifacts from the nineteenth century, and maritime displays are in abundance on account of Polson's proximity to Flathead Lake.

Speaking of Flathead Lake, there is one very ugly, bony creature mounted to a wall, with a plaque stating its identity as being the

★ ★

Flathead Monster. Flossie, as she is known in these parts, bears a striking resemblance to a 7-foot, 6-inch white sturgeon.

Another of the more notable attractions is Calamity Jane's saddle. It was procured from Terry, South Dakota, where the famed sharp-shooter took her last ride.

As you stroll through the museum (and its yard, which contains buggies, wagons, and an old trading post), you'll find an unending number of fascinating photos, displays, and items from Montana's long and colorful history.

But for sheer curiosity impact, you can't beat the marionettes: those rosy-cheeked, loose-limbed historical characters gathered around the fake campfire, seeming to plot the next day's course on their Pacific-seeking adventure in their fringed buckskin and fur hats. Just don't call them puppets.

The Polson-Flathead Historical Museum is located at 708 Main Street, downtown Polson. Open during the summer months, their hours are from 9 a.m. to 5 p.m., Monday through Saturday, and from 12 to 3 p.m. on Sunday. Their phone number is (406) 883-3049, and their Web site is www.polsonflatheadmuseum.org.

He Ain't Heavy, He's My Hippo
Polson

"Just so everybody knows, I don't know what I'm doing and we all may die." So begins a run on the *Happy Hippo* in Polson, with Capt. Bob Ricketts announcing from the bridge. Or is it a cockpit? Or the driver's seat? In the *Happy Hippo*'s case, it's all three.

The ten-ton amphibious vehicle, painted up and outfitted for fun on the water, carries a load of tourists out into Flathead Lake twice a day in the summer. Ricketts, who owns Three Dog Down and Three Dog Adventure Tours, can usually be found at the controls of the *Hippo*, making sure all passengers get completely soaked when the vehicle plunges into the lake. And if he's not piloting that vehicle, he'll be riding a waverunner in the lake, leading a horde of pirates as

★ ★

they swarm the *Hippo*, drenching its occupants with water guns.

The *Hippo* is not about to give in, however, and easily repels the pirate attacks with a huge water cannon that continually knocks the bogus buccaneers off their boats into the chilly waters of Flathead Lake.

In summer, the *Happy Hippo* is on the run every day, getting a full load of tourists soaked to the bone for $15 a pop. Ricketts hires local kids to don dreadlocks and bandanas and terrorize the *Hippo* with plastic knives in their teeth, and he leads these waterborne raids with the gusto of an adolescent with permission to squirt.

The fun-loving entrepreneur acquired the Vietnam-era LARC (Lighter Amphibious Resupply Cargo) from the Dayton Volunteer Fire Department, which wasn't crazy about the expensive maintenance on the

If the navy had painted all their watercraft
to look like this, the Vietnam War would
have been over in ten minutes.

★ ★

unique vehicle. Powered by a Cummins 903 diesel V8, the *Hippo* can get its 4-foot-tall tires rolling at up to 30 miles per hour, which makes for a bumpy ride on account of the vehicle's lack of suspension.

But when you're tooling down the Polson Beach boat ramp and plunge into the lake at that speed, it creates a massive wall of water that crashes back down over the boat in a dramatic drenching you won't see anywhere this side of Disneyland.

Happy Hippo rides are offered twice a day from Three Dog Adventures, on the west side of the Armed Forces Memorial Bridge in Polson. Call (800) 364-3696 for more information.

It Just Needs a Coat of Dutch Boy Paint
Ravalli

The tiny hamlet of Ravalli, where MT 200 shoots west off of US 93, is a fairly unremarkable little town. Its historical claim to fame is probably the Great Buffalo Roundup of 1906. You can stop and have a pretty decent buffalo burger, but most people blow right through on their way to Flathead Lake, or maybe the National Bison Range in Moiese.

But if you keep your eyes peeled and watch the west side of the railroad tracks, you may see something that will cause you to ask, as Bugs Bunny did, if you should have turned left at Albuquerque. Right there next to a little trout-filled pond, big as life, is a five-story Dutch windmill.

Upon closer inspection, though, you might surmise that it doesn't look Dutch at all. Oh, it's got the big, four-bladed wooden fan. But the actual building looks a lot like an old tipi burner. And that's exactly what it is.

When the sawmill that once occupied the site burned down in the 1960s, the steel, tipi-shaped burner was left standing. Rather than dismantle and dispose of it, which was prohibitively expensive, the new owners decided to transform it into a Dutch windmill and turn it into a bed and breakfast.

A St. Ignatius contractor was hired to make the exterior transformation, and the inside was gutted and remodeled to feature a large kitchen, laundry facilities, and several bedrooms. Fire code regulations would have required an escape ladder out of each window, though, and the owners couldn't bear to have the sleek exterior ruined by such an abomination. Their bed and breakfast dreams up in smoke, they sold out and retired to Arizona.

The current owners have refurbished the windmill into a conventional (relatively speaking) home, and have opened a café right next door. Windmill Village is famous for their donuts, and their pies will make you think you've died and gone to heaven. Just make sure you leave your wooden shoes at the door.

Windmill Village is located in Ravalli, just south of the MT 200 interchange. Call (406) 745-2270 to learn more.

The Original Jerky Boys
Rollins

It sits quietly near the western shore of Flathead Lake, this unassuming, sixty-year-old building. Ravens and magpies flit among the statuesque ponderosa pines that surround it, and the little country store seems to be like every other Mom-and-Pop joint between Whitefish and Hamilton.

But walk through the front door of M & S Meats & Sausage and you'll enter a vegetarian's worst nightmare. The carved buffalo on the front porch might offer a clue as to its specialty.

In the coolers at the back of the small store, you'll find all manner of meats, including cuts coming from buffalo, elk, antelope, cattle, chicken, turkey, and pigs. The various species are ground into sausage, dried into jerky, or cut into thick steaks. You'll also find buffalo and elk salami, as well as smoked salmon, ox tails for stew, and Thuringer elk. They're also known for their honey-cured hams and low-fat pork sausage.

M & S Meats & Sausage also sells several varieties of local wine,

★ ★

huckleberry treats from the surrounding mountains, and cherry con-
fections from the Flathead orchards.

Easily the most popular item, though, is M & S's buffalo jerky.
They create it in four varieties: jalapeño, teriyaki, pepper, and original. It's shipped all over the world, and according to employee Leanor
Jaeger, in the summer they need to hang an average of 700 pounds
of buffalo a day just to keep up with the demand.

And if repulsing vegetarians isn't enough, their quality selection
of exotic and smoked cheeses should keep vegans moving down the
road as well.

Sonny and Lucy Carlson are the owners, and I asked a young man
behind the counter what the M & S stands for in the store's name.

"Meats and Sausage," he said with a straight face.

M & S Meats & Sausage is located at 86755 US 93 South in
Rollins. To feed your inner carnivore, call (406) 844-3414 or visit
www.msmeats.com.

In Ronan, a Museum Full of Old Things
Ronan

There are some 230 museums in Montana, and it seems that the
further removed from the mainstream they are, the more interesting
they become.

Take Ronan's Garden of the Rockies Museum, for example. Like
most of the more intimate museums in Montana, this one takes most
of its displays from local donors, and is a deep reflection on the particular way of life found in the area. In Ronan, that means farming.

The grounds are crowded with ancient farming machinery and
implements, rusted from decades of disuse. Nearly all of the carts,
plows, and wagons are of the horse-drawn variety. There are a couple of old tractors, but next to all the other ancient gear, they look
like spaceships.

Inside the building, which was originally the first Catholic church in
Ronan, remnants of yesteryear paint a vivid picture of a hardscrabble

yet occasionally sophisticated life in this little town at the south end of the Flathead Valley. Ronan's first telephone switchboard is there, dating from the 1930s. You'll also find a display packed with vintage dental tools and instruments, including the leather-upholstered chair that held the quivering patients.

Dozens of high school yearbooks from area schools line one shelf, some dating back to the 1940s. There are all kinds of ladies' pillbox hats displayed on Styrofoam heads that have all had thin eyebrows carefully painted on. No other facial features, mind you, just eyebrows.

One fascinating item is a very well-preserved Wurlitzer Simplex Multi-Selector, a complex machine that plays 78s, selected according to a dizzying dial of buttons on the front. It's obviously a precursor to the jukebox, and you have to wonder what it was doing out here on the prairie.

When you leave the museum, make sure you stop by the Sloans Flat Stage Stop, which has been moved and rebuilt next to the main building. Originally constructed in 1885, the stage stop is outfitted and furnished to look like it's frozen in time, right down to the poker game in progress on the table inside. The room is encircled with dozens of fine, vintage cowboy hats, presumably belonging to men who knew when to hold 'em, and when to fold 'em.

Ronan's Garden of the Rockies Museum can be found at 400 Round Butte Road West. They're open from mid-April to Labor Day. Try calling (406) 676-5210 for more information.

Generations of Collecting in One Museum
Ronan

Bud Cheff Sr. grew up with the Indians in the lower Flathead Valley, and his childhood sowed the seeds for one of the most interesting— but most overlooked—museums in Montana.

The Ninepipes Museum of Early Montana is a huge, sweeping collection of artifacts, artworks, and historical displays that tell the story of life in western Montana 150 years ago. Cheff began collecting

Indian artifacts and other items when he was a young boy, and today his collection is augmented by over 1,000 other items of everyday life from area Native Americans and white settlers.

Artworks of Charlie Russell, E. S. Paxson, and other western masters are on display in the Gallery of Art of the Old West, and you can view hundreds of period images in the Hall of Photographs. Dozens of displays show off original Indian clothing and tools used by the Nez Perce, Pend d'Oreille, and Salish tribes in the Flathead Valley.

The stunning centerpiece of the museum is the Indian diorama, a life-size tableau that depicts a typical Indian encampment. There's a buckskin tipi, circa 1889, and a rack of drying buffalo meat. A native woman is scraping a buffalo hide while children play. During the frequent tours given to groups of local schoolchildren, Cheff has been known to creep inside the tipi and beat on a hand drum while singing an ancient tribal song he learned as a boy at the knees of Indian elders. It's a powerful moment, and it never fails to affect the kids lucky enough to witness the scene.

The museum's gift shop is packed with Indian items, some authentic and some expertly crafted replicas. There's also a well-stocked book corner, and plenty of jewelry and gifts. You'll also see a buffalo skull for sale ($285), as well as an authentic pair of beaded Sioux moccasins ($1,250).

The Ninepipes Museum of Early Montana is a treasure trove of history, not to be missed if you're traveling through the area. Make sure you've got several hours, though, as you'll no doubt be transported back in time by the fascinating displays and the powerful, gripping story of Indians and settlers sharing the beauty of the Flathead Valley.

The Ninepipes Museum of Early Montana is located at 40962 US 93 North near Charlo. They're open seven days a week from Memorial Day through Labor Day, from 8 a.m. to 6 p.m. In the slow season, they are open Wednesday through Sunday, from 11 a.m. to 5 p.m. Special tours can be arranged with advance notice. Call (406) 644-3435 or visit www.ninepipes.org.

It's More Than Just Arrowheads—Way More
St. Ignatius

Preston E. Miller (along with his partner, Carolyn Corey) is one of the nation's foremost authorities on Native American artifacts. His *Four Winds Guide to Indian Trade Goods and Replicas* is a best-selling handbook for identifying historical and archeological items of the western American Indian culture. So you would expect his Four Winds Trading Post to be chock full of Indian items.

And you would be right. Montana's oldest continually operating trading post may appear somewhat unassuming from the exterior,

Sorry, little brown jugs not available in the gift shop.

★ ★

but the Four Winds Trading Post is a seemingly endless collection of all things Indian, with a healthy dose of pioneer and explorer history, focusing on the western migration of the mid- to late-1800s.

The trading post building itself is the original structure built by Duncan McDonald, a "factor," or proprietor, for the Hudson's Bay Company. Miller's collection is heavy with HBC items, from wooden shipping crates to engraved glassware.

But this collection is nothing if not eclectic. Miller procured the original Ravalli Great Northern Railway depot, and had it moved to this spot in the lower Flathead Valley. Inside the depot he's stockpiled entire rooms full of Great Northern paraphernalia, from railroad signals and signs right down to the original depot office.

Deep inside the huge train depot, Miller shows off his collection of military swords. He also has two large rooms stuffed with hundreds and hundreds of model trains. He's even got a standard-gauge model of the rare "Blue Comet" running around on a detailed track, along with two more trains of different gauges.

Another building on the grounds is the original cabin where Mary Finley was born. She and her little brother were the only two survivors of the infamous Swan Valley Massacre of 1908. The original Jocko Indian Agency building, circa 1862, stands nearby, complete with the original fireplace constructed of adobe bricks.

Back in the original trading post building, Miller happily supplies stories and historical facts to visitors while they poke around among the Indian medicinal herbs, beading supplies, hundreds of books on Indian and western culture, and handcrafted replica artifacts. There's even an ancient stereoscope machine that, for a quarter, shows in stark detail the Great Buffalo Roundup of 1906, which took place in nearby Ravalli. You can even see the depot in its original setting in most of the photos.

Preston Miller's Four Winds Trading Post is located on US 93 North, 3 miles north of St. Ignatius. They are open daily from 9 a.m. to 5 p.m. in the summer, and from 12 to 5 p.m. in the winter. Call (406) 745-4336 for more information.

Fort Connah: Oldest Standing Building in Montana. Maybe.
St. Ignatius

Imagine this real estate ad: "Cozee fronteer charmher, big ol view of Mission MoUntins, neer Mullan Trail. 4 Sail by Bilder. If You aint afeered of Blackfeets, fine opprtnty 4 trappers or sod bustters. Cash on the Barrelhed perfered."

Such might have been the description of Fort Connah, the oldest standing building in Montana (or is the oldest building in Fort Benton? See "The Oldest Building in Montana. Probably." in chapter 6). Built in 1847 by Angus McDonald, the structure was not a military fort but rather a small complex of buildings that served as a trading post (or factory, as it was called) for the Hudson's Bay Company. McDonald traded dried buffalo meat, blankets, furs, rawhide cords, and other necessities with Indians and white travelers alike.

Located on US 93 about 6 miles north of St. Ignatius, Fort Connah was finally opened to public access in the spring of 2009, after being closed since 1871. The Fort Connah Restoration Society has been working to restore and refurbish the original building to its 1850s appearance. Several outbuildings have been reconstructed to their original specifications, using historical drawings and photographs to ensure their accuracy.

Angus McDonald, who was reportedly something of a wild man, would probably have approved of the rendezvous that's held each year at Fort Connah. History buffs and modern-day mountain men don their buckskin outfits, pitch their period-correct wall tents on the site, and spend the weekend having tomahawk-throwing and archery exhibitions. They also share with visitors their knowledge and passion of the pioneer days in the Flathead Valley.

The fort building is the main attraction, though, and it is still more than 90 percent original. The interior has been painstakingly restored and outfitted to reflect the harsh, demanding life of a factor running this isolated trading post on the desolate prairie of nineteenth-century Montana. There's an antique spinning wheel in the corner, several ancient cooking vessels arranged on shelves, and the walls are covered with various animal pelts, as well as several photographs showing what the area looked like 150 years ago.

To find Fort Connah, look for the sign on US 93 North, about 6 miles north of St. Ignatius. You can see the buildings from the highway.

All They Need Is a Grizzly With a Credit Card
St. Ignatius

So you're tooling down US 93 North, wondering if there's anywhere in St. Ignatius to snag a refreshing huckleberry ice cream cone. You see, the huckleberry is to Montana as the pineapple is to Hawaii: This is where we grow them, and the closer to the source you get them, the more delicious they are.

Fortunately, there is indeed a place along US 93 where all your huckleberry dreams can come true. A former fruit stand outside of St. Ignatius has been reborn as the Huckleberry Jam Factory, and they not only offer the aforementioned huckleberry ice cream cones (soft serve), but they'll be happy to whip up a huckleberry shake if that's your preference.

Hands chapped from holding that huckleberry cone while you ride your Harley down the highway? Better pick up a bottle of huckleberry lotion. It'll go great with the huckleberry bath beads and huckleberry soap that will make you the target of every bear within 20 miles of your next backwoods hike.

There are several varieties of huckleberry jam, of course, as well as jelly, ice cream topping, taffy, vinaigrette salad dressing, huckleberry chocolate cordials, and huckleberry infused coffee beans.

There are a few items that don't feature the mighty purple mountain fruit, like Indian fry bread mix, local raspberries, and freshly pressed apple cider, but you can buy that stuff anywhere. At the Huckleberry Jam Factory, the huckleberry is king.

The Huckleberry Jam Factory is located at 1 Museum Lane, next to the Doug Allard's Flathead Indian Museum on US 93 North, St. Ignatius. They're open from April until October, and can be reached at (406) 745-2951.

The Closest You'll Get Without Getting Wet

St. Regis

Montana is famous for its large concentration of blue-ribbon trout streams, and its lakes and rivers are still teeming with world-record specimens of the salmonid family. But there's only one place where you'll find huge rainbows, brookies, and cutthroats within a few yards of a jackalope, a guitar-playing bear, and a pair of slippers shaped like cowboy boots.

The St. Regis Travel Center boasts a well-stocked trout aquarium at the back of its 6,000-square-foot gift shop. You can get yourself

I think it's fair to say these trout have never missed a meal.

face to face with a 28-inch rainbow trout, and feel the scorn as he stares at you from his temperature-controlled enclosure. Some of these bad boys have been around a few years, and the bigger ones have developed the hooked jaw, the bulging forehead, and the menacing scowl that would seem to make them prime candidates for extras in a Martin Scorsese movie.

Trout like it cold, from the mid-50s to about 62 degrees, and the six large tanks are kept at a constant temperature to keep the fish lively and active. It's really a great opportunity to get up close and personal with Montana's favorite fish.

The centerpiece of the trout display is a circular aquarium set at eye level (well, if you're ten years old). There's an opening in the base that you can crawl through, and then you can stand up in the center of this fish-filled donut to find yourself surrounded by large trout swimming endless laps around you. It makes for a pretty good photo op.

The St. Regis Travel Center also features a restaurant and casino, and while you're in the gift shop, keep your eyes peeled for Barry Wild and the Drifters, an animatronic band of forest creatures that springs to life every fifteen minutes to play a song. Barry, on guitar, is joined by a keyboard-playing wolf and a moose behind the drum kit. The juxtaposition between the natural and the unnatural is almost surreal, but when the Drifters snap into action, the trout seem to pick up their pace, undulating in time with the music.

Or maybe that's just the huckleberry smoothie going to my head.

The St. Regis Travel Center is just off exit 33 on I-90. Call (866) 649-2407 to learn more.

Dude, Where's My Train?
Somers

Oh, it must have been a startling sight: Old Number 215, the steam engine out of Kalispell, rolling backwards down the track for 11 miles into Somers, where it smashed through a tool shed before plunging into the frigid waters of Flathead Lake.

Somebody forgot to set the emergency brake.

The year was 1908, and Engine 215 of the Great Northern Railway was scheduled for its regular run from Kalispell to Somers. The usual engineer, though, was sick. He was replaced on this day by Otto Fenske, a fireman. To the best recollection of witnesses and Fenske's own account, here's what happened:

Fenske jumped off the engine to close the switch in the track, and the engine slipped into reverse and started moving backwards down the track. Fenske couldn't catch it, and so watched helplessly as the engine accelerated into a full, 140-pound head of steam, and lumbered out of sight toward Somers.

As the train passed the depot in Somers without so much as a howdy-do, it entered a steep grade in the track that led down to a dock on the shoreline. Engine 215 hurtled down the track and shot out onto the dock, smashing through a tool shed before splashing into 20 feet of Flathead Lake water. It's estimated that the engine traveled 40 feet through the air before splashing down.

The dock was not only repaired but fortified. It needed to be able to support the seventy-five-ton crane that was used to retrieve the engine from the bottom of the lake. You can see the battered runaway now, cleaned up and proudly displayed at the trailhead of the Great Northern Historic Trail in Somers. Local news accounts of the incident are posted at a kiosk, along with historic photos and more local information.

Engine 215 is on display on Somers Road, about four blocks east of US 93 North.

Fort Owen: Stevensville's Window to the Past
Stevensville

You might think that the oldest white settlement in Montana might be that family who's been hogging the primo campsite across from the island on Lake Alva. But no. The official "oldest settlement" goes to Fort Owen in the Bitterroot Valley.

Fort Owen State Park is a small but history-packed collection of buildings and artifacts of the original fort, which was established in 1850 by John Owen, a trader from the U.S. Army. Owen purchased the St. Mary's Mission, which had been operated since the 1840s by Jesuit missionaries. The Jesuits had grown wheat, oats, and potatoes, but once the mission changed hands, Owen converted it into a trading post. St. Mary's was reestablished in Stevensville some sixteen years later.

The grist mill and sawmill built by the Jesuits remained in use at the fort, increasing its importance to the residents of the valley. When the discovery of gold in the Bannack area brought a rush of

★ ★

settlers to the area in the 1860s, Fort Owen became an important resource for the miners.

Very little of the original fort is still there, but the replica buildings and interpretive kiosks are top notch, delivering the look and feel of mid-nineteenth-century Montana. There is an original log cabin, built in the 1870s, that was moved to the site to add another dimension to the period representation. The cabin was the original home of John Wagner, one of three brothers who emigrated from Germany to the Bitterroot Valley in 1867. The cabin is furnished in the style of the era, and has informational displays inside.

The centerpiece of Fort Owen State Park is the adobe-brick barracks building, which houses several rooms of artifacts and informational panels. There are also some detailed scale models of the original Fort Owen.

You can stand outside, near the spot of the original front wall of the fort, and almost imagine the fur traders, the Blackfeet marauders, and the pioneer settlers moving through the area, all thinking the same thing: "I wonder if there's a KOA around here?"

Fort Owen State Park is about 1 mile east of US 93 South, near Stevensville.

Seems Like 'On the Road' Would Have Been More Appropriate
Superior

We've all seen one in the drawer of the hotel nightstand. The Gideon's Bible has been acknowledged in songs by Frank Zappa, Jimmy Buffet, and the Beatles, and it's become a well-known cultural icon for travelers. Standard equipment in hotels and motels everywhere, the very first free copies of the Good Book were placed in a Superior, Montana, hotel in 1908.

The Gideons International was founded in 1899 by two Christian men who had met the previous year at the Central Hotel in Boscobel, Wisconsin. In their early years the Gideons was a group comprised of almost all traveling men. In an effort to maximize the effectiveness of their witnesses in the hotels where they stayed, the Gideons began furnishing a copy of the Bible for each hotel room. The national Ministerial Union agreed to provide the funds for these Bibles, and they were off to the races. "The Bible Project," as it was called, was also seen as a gracious undertaking in keeping with the divine mission of the Gideon Association.

Superior became the first recipient of Gideon's Bibles when Archie Bailey, a Gideon who worked nearby and was a frequent guest at the Superior Hotel, approached Mrs. Edna Wilkinson, who ran the joint, and asked permission to place Bibles in the rooms. She agreed, and Bailey sent an order to the Gideon headquarters in Chicago, along with a personal donation to cover the costs.

The original Superior Hotel burned down in 1940, but its replacement sits on a rise on the northeast edge of town, overlooking a beautiful section of the Clark Fork River. On a gloomy day, the now-defunct hotel looks pretty creepy, like the kind of place where Anthony Perkins might rent you a room. Caretakers have kept the building up over the years, though, and its historic significance remains, attracting hundreds of curiosity-seekers each year.

And it's a good thing the Gideons created this generous tradition. Imagine if the Beatles had sung, "Rocky Raccoon checked into his room, only to find a month-old copy of the *National Enquirer*."

Schneider's Garage stands on the site of the original hotel, and there is a plaque commemorating the first Gideon's Bible. The Superior Hotel is located on the northeast end of town.

How Low Can You Go?
Troy

Montana is spread out over the northern end of the American Rockies, straddling the Continental Divide, the "backbone" of the continent. That means we're up there in the thin air, looking down on the rest of the country. Or maybe the rest of the country looks up to us; yeah, that sounds better. We're thousands of feet closer to the sun than our friends in Seattle or Miami—so don't look down! The highest point in Montana is Granite Peak, just north of Yellowstone Park in the Beartooth Mountains. It's well over 2 miles above sea level, at 12,799 feet. Parking is scarce. If you feel like strapping on the crampons and braving ice walls and jagged rocks in order to reach that peak, hey, knock yourself out. Write if you find work.

But if you'd like to experience the other extreme and stand at the lowest point in the state, it's a bit easier: You just have to pull off US 2 at the Idaho border. Right there, where the Kootenai River flows into the Idaho panhandle, you'll be standing at a mere 1,800 feet above sea level. Okay, to be honest, you're probably closer to 1,900 feet because the river is down below you in a forested valley. But, hey—you don't have to tell that to your friends in Seattle and Miami when you send them the photo of yourself bottoming out by the "Welcome to Idaho" sign.

The lowest point in Montana is on US 2 at the Idaho border, just northwest of Troy. It's open twenty-four hours. Ha-ha.

Bridge Over Bubbled Waters
Troy

If you have a problem with heights or fast-moving water, skip ahead to the next chapter right now. But if you seek cheap thrills and enjoy having your heart rate elevated by fear and panic, I've got just the place for you.

It's the swinging bridge over the Kootenai River, just downstream from Kootenai Falls. After walking along the trail system through the 135-acre Kootenai Falls Park, you take the route that leads to a concrete bridge spanning a pair of railroad tracks. Then it's a short hike through a sun-dappled forest to the bridge.

It's not as precarious as it looks, despite the sign that warns of a five-person maximum. It's tethered by thick steel cables that prevent it from swinging too much; but let me tell you, it swings enough. You walk out onto the 3-foot-wide bridge and, as the wind comes

If sleeping on the top bunk makes you nervous,
I'd steer clear of this baby.

whipping down the river canyon, even the bravest explorers will be tightly gripping the handrails. It's about a 60-foot drop to the churning water (judging by the three seconds it took for my loogie to hit the river).

In the spring and early summer, the Libby Dam upstream releases huge amounts of water from Lake Koocanusa, turning the rushing,

★ ★

roiling river the color of avocado flesh. The cables that actually support the bridge are nearly an inch thick, but once you get out to the middle of the thing, it's still nerve-wracking enough that a surprise train whistle can cause you to soil yourself.

On that note, restrooms are available at the trailhead near the parking lot. Better visit them before you walk to the bridge.

The swinging bridge over the Kootenai River is at milepost 21 on US 2, between Troy and Libby. The trail to the bridge is not wheelchair accessible.

They've Got the Simple Bear Necessities
West Glacier

Montana has its own version of Jurassic Park tucked into the woods just west of Glacier Park. I imagine they wanted to call it Bearassic Park, but thankfully they resisted that temptation. Instead, it's known as the Great Bear Adventure. "Your Car Is Your Cage!" is emblazoned on the big roadside sign. Holy velociraptor!

After you pay your fee to enter the drive-through bear park, you are bombarded with a stern list of rules that threaten imminent danger and violence from the large, free-roaming beasts: "Stay in your

Trivia

Three men died during the construction of Going-to-the-Sun Road in Glacier Park, a project that took twenty years. Plans for Going-to-Helena Handbasket State Highway are still in the works.

★ ★

car at all times. Doors must be locked and windows closed. Do not feed or tempt bears. Do not let bears touch your vehicle."

As you roll slowly into the sylvan setting, you will soon see several large, well-fed black bears moving through the twenty-four-acre park, which is surrounded by an electrified fence. We all know how effective that fence was against a T-rex, but it seems big enough to contain these fearsome creatures.

Well, maybe "fearsome" is a bit strong. After all the warnings and rules, it's a little surprising to see some dude in cargo shorts and

Your car is your cage.

sandals walking around among the bears, carrying a large bucket of Purina Bear Chow. He stops periodically to dump a pile of kibble, and the bears follow him around like overgrown Labradors, pausing occasionally to scrape at a lodgepole pine or splash around in one of the large, cement ponds.

The place really seems more like a minimum-security prison than a wild animal park. The only difference? The inmates are all male black bears that have been raised in captivity. The park no longer has grizzly bears, presumably because two employees have been attacked by the ill-tempered predators since 2004.

Still, it's a kick to see a 700-pound black bear walk right by your car. Just don't let him see your picnic basket, or he and his buddy Boo-Boo might block the exit.

Great Bear Adventure is located right along US 2 East, between Coram and West Glacier.

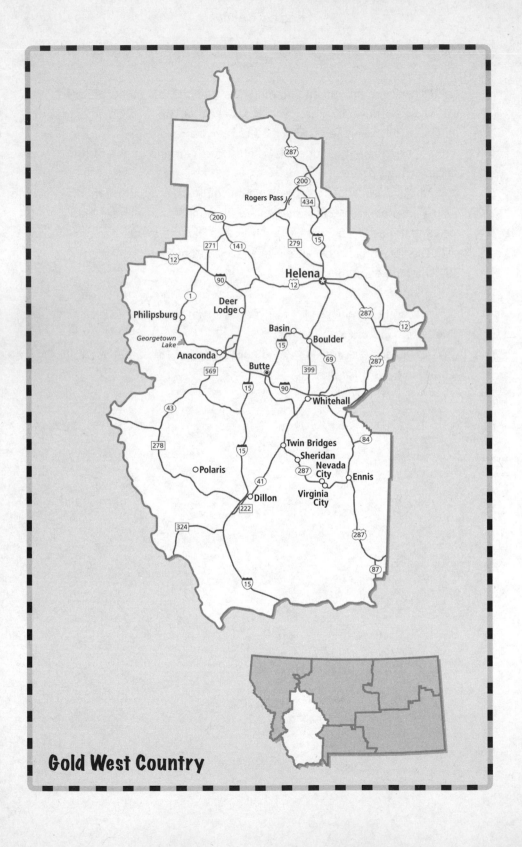

Gold West Country

2

Gold West Country

"Oro y Plata," *Montana's state slogan, means "silver and gold." The importance of the mining and smelting of gold, silver, and copper in Montana cannot be overstated, and nowhere is the history more evident than in Gold West Country.*

The twin ghost towns of Nevada City and Virginia City are packed with living history, still showing vestiges of Montana's gold rush of the 1880s, including their own Boot Hill cemetery and Club Foot George's actual club foot. The world's largest brick smokestack, which was used in smelting copper, still stands in Anaconda. That town, in fact, would have been the state capital were it not for some hinky vote counting that tipped the decision in Helena's favor.

And then there's Butte, the Richest Hill on Earth. Their St. Patrick's Day celebration is widely known, but precious few have ever heard of St. Uhro's Day, which takes place there the day before.

Helena, like Butte, celebrates its gold mining heritage with tours, museums, and landmarks dedicated to the gold-fevered miners, and to the funky and sometimes puzzling evidence of their lives in the Last Chance Gulch. The architecture, public art, and city events are heavily influenced by those who struck it rich. At the height of Helena's gold frenzy, the city had more millionaires per capita than anywhere on earth.

So grab your pickax and gold pan, and dig into some weird history, goofy artifacts, and just plain curious attractions in Montana's Gold West Country.

Art Deco Lives at Club Moderne

Anaconda

In a smelting town full of one-hundred-year-old buildings, the Club Moderne stands out like a narc at a Grateful Dead concert. The flashy, art-deco building is one of a few structures in Anaconda that flaunt the popular style from the 1920s.

With the U.S. mired in the Great Depression, working stiffs were desperate for distraction, and in 1937 the Club Moderne delivered it in spades. Opened with a gala celebration on October 9, John

A seventy-five-year-old bar named Club Moderne.
How about a tall frosty glass of irony?

★ ★

"Skinny" Francisco's opulent bar was an immediate hit. The art-deco style, which had been introduced in Paris in 1925, ignored classic architectural references in favor of clean, swooping, geometric lines that reflected the burgeoning industrial age.

Club Moderne was designed by Bozeman architect Fred Willson, and constructed by Theodore Eck of Anaconda. It was finished and outfitted entirely by local craftsmen, who took obvious pride in this jewel of the elbow-bending set. Smooth Carrara glass panels envelope the rounded façade, set off by long lines of neon.

The well-preserved interior boasts lots of chrome and leather, replete with inlaid wood and Formica tables. In this sleek, sophisticated atmosphere, it doesn't take much imagination to transport yourself back to the time of Betty Boop, the Lindy Hop, and mandatory hats.

The Club Moderne was listed in the National Register of Historic Places in 1986. It's located at 801 East Park Avenue in Anaconda. Call (406) 563-9915 to get a taste of a bygone age.

When Bridget Got the Ax, All She Lost Was Her Job
Anaconda

Lizzie Borden took an ax
And gave her mother forty whacks,
When she saw what she had done
She gave her father forty-one.

Sure, it's some gruesome prose, but is it any worse than any Grimm Brothers tale? This well-known poem refers to one of the more sensational crimes in modern times. The brutal double murder of Lizzie Borden's parents was shocking news, and it made major headlines across the country. To this day, no one knows the full truth of what went down that day over one hundred years ago.

It was a Thursday morning in August of 1892 when Bridget

Sullivan, the maid, was told by Mrs. Borden to wash the windows of their house in Fall River, Massachusetts. After cleaning the kitchen from breakfast, Bridget went outside with a washbasin to begin the sloppy task. She didn't see Lizzie Borden during this time, because Lizzie was in a second-floor guest room, hacking her stepmother to death with a hatchet.

Ninety minutes later, as Bridget rested in her attic room, Mr. Borden was sprawled on the sitting room couch, also dead from several deep ax wounds. Was it Lizzie? Or was it Bridget?

Bridget Sullivan, whom the Borden family all called "Maggie," had arrived in the U.S. from her native Ireland in 1886, and was hired on as the Bordens' house servant. After the murder trial she moved to Anaconda, where she was employed as a domestic. She married John M. Sullivan, a smeltman, in 1905.

Bridget's presence in the Borden home on the morning of the horrific double murder added a layer of mystery to the question of Lizzie Borden's guilt. Since she was not an eyewitness to the brutal acts, she could only testify as to the whereabouts of everyone who was home that morning, and her testimony contradicted much of Lizzie's.

Even though Lizzie had attempted to buy some powerful poison from the druggist the day before, and her story kept changing during the investigation, her father was not well liked in the community and the jury at her trial acquitted her of the murders.

Her life largely a mystery, and with no definitive answers to the crime yet offered, Lizzie Borden remains one of the most compelling characters in American crime lore. How could such a well-bred young woman commit such a heinous crime? How could she get away with it? What really happened that morning 120 years ago?

If Bridget Sullivan knew the answers to any of those questions, she took them with her to her grave in 1948. She's still there, overlooking the quiet town of Anaconda.

Bridget Sullivan's grave is located in the Olivet Hill section of the Anaconda cemetery.

★ ★

Almost One Hundred Years Old, Probably Because She Quit Smoking

Anaconda

You can see it all the way from Deer Lodge, 25 miles away, looming up in the foothills like a black toothpick of death. But as you turn off onto MT 1 and head west toward Anaconda, the Washoe Smokestack is revealed to be a massive, 585-foot-tall tower of black-bricked beauty.

Built in 1918 as part of the Washoe Smelter where copper was processed, the Stack (as it's known locally) is the world's largest freestanding brick structure. The top is 60 feet in diameter, and the bottom is 75 feet across. It's big enough to be used as a packing crate for the Washington Monument, although some FedEx size restrictions may apply.

Residents of Anaconda, Butte, and other nearby towns revere the stack as a monument to the area's rich history in mining and smelting. In Laurie Mercier's book, *Anaconda: Labor, Community and Culture in Montana's Smelter City*, Anaconda historian Bob Vine put it succinctly: "Everybody would get up in the morning and look to see if there was smoke coming out of the stack, and if there was, God was in His heaven and all was right with the world and we knew we were going to have a paycheck."

The stack is listed on the National Register of Historic Places, and was deeded to the state by the Atlantic Richfield Company. Plans to demolish the stack in 1985 were thwarted by the efforts of Anaconda residents, who have come to love the structure as a powerful reminder of their blue-collar history and proud mining tradition. It stands amidst several mountainous piles of slag, the black sand that was a byproduct of the smelting process.

The numbers involved in the construction of the smokestack and its 30-foot high octagonal base are staggering: 62,000 sacks of cement, 127 railroad cars of sand, 118 cars of crushed rock, and who knows how many trips to Home Depot. The stack itself contains

Taller than the Washington Monument.
And less pointy.

★ ★

2,464,672 tile blocks, the equivalent of 6,672,214 ordinary bricks. Workers built the stack in 142 days, and it still stands there on Smelter Hill at the edge of town, towering 1,000 feet over Anaconda.

When environmental stabilization of the stack is complete, visitors will be allowed to go right up to the base. But for now, an interpretive site is located at Benny Goodman Park, practically in the shadow of the stack. The site features a ground-level replica of the uppermost 4 feet of the stack, which holds a quantity of black slag. There are also several markers and informational kiosks.

The Washoe Stack is visible along US 1, on the east end of Anaconda. I know people say this all the time, but honestly, you can't miss it.

Even the Popcorn Is Gold-Plated
Anaconda

Anaconda is home to a theater so beautiful that you might spend more time looking at its lavish appointments than watching the screen. Don't let the unassuming exterior fool you—the Washoe Theater is one of the top three most beautiful historic theaters still in use in the U.S., as designated by the Smithsonian Institute.

The Washoe sits on the site of the original Margaret Theatre, which burned down in 1929. Constructed at a cost of $200,000, the Washoe's opening was delayed by the onset of the Great Depression, and didn't take its first tickets until 1936. It was designed by B. Marcus Priteca of Seattle, who also designed the Coliseum for that city. Huge, elaborate movie theaters were the order of the day, but the magnificent Washoe made most of them look like tarpaper shacks in comparison.

The interior of the Washoe is simply spectacular, a testament to the area's significant gold and copper industries. Eight shades of gold decorate the stage pilasters and proscenium, which are accented in copper leaf. The walls hold several intricate murals, some with genuine gold leaf backgrounds. Elegant light fixtures gently illuminate the

★ ★

hallways, and carved ram heads line the ceiling. A huge mural dominates the dome overhead in the main theater. Entitled *Montana*, the
mural depicts the many ways in which civilization depends upon copper. According to theater employee Dianna Kellie, the nude women
in the mural were removed or had clothing painted on at some point.

The theater is designed and appointed in a lavish art nouveau
style, and is complemented by a more art deco look in the lobby and
exterior. The 968-seat facility boasts an actual silver screen, which is
expensive to repair and maintain. The hand-painted curtains depict
rearing deer in gold and red against a turquoise background. The
Washoe hosts the occasional live production on its full-size stage,
and still shows movies with the original 1936 Simplex projectors and
original speakers.

The Washoe Theater is located at 305 Main Street in Anaconda.
Call (406) 563-6161 for more information.

Mmm . . . Radiation!
Boulder/Basin

According to the EPA Web site, radon is a cancer-causing, naturally
radioactive gas that you can't see, smell, or taste. Its presence in your
home can be dangerous to your health, and it's second only to ciga-
rette smoking as a cause of lung cancer in America. So if you discovered that your hard rock gold mine was suddenly emitting huge levels
of radon, what would you do?

Well, if you were in the Boulder/Basin area in the early 1950s,
you'd open a health spa and charge people three bucks a pop to visit
the dank caves and breathe the carcinogenic fumes.

That's what's happened at four different spots in this little corner
of the state between Helena and Butte. All the businesses have such
happy names: the Earth Angel Mine, the Sunshine Health Mine, the
Free Enterprise, the Merry Widow. People come from all over the world
because they swear that the radon "treatments" cure their ills, which
range from arthritis to eczema to lupus. They feel that these short

Hundreds of people a year go into this
radon mine. On purpose.

★ ★

exposures (one or two hours) to these high levels of radon (175 times higher than the federal "oh crap!" level) are not unlike an organic version of radiation therapy. It zaps the bad but leaves the good.

Migraines, cataracts, fibromyalgia, asthma, even multiple sclerosis have all been treated by radon enthusiasts who spend hours sitting in the mines, playing checkers, reading books, or working on needlepoint. It's a little creepy to walk hundreds of feet under a mountain through a rugged tunnel only to come across a little old lady on a bench, flipping through a large-print *Reader's Digest* like she's waiting for a bus.

Three radon health mines are located in the Basin area, and one is in Boulder. The Earth Angel Mine is open year-round. Call (406) 225-3516 to get dosed.

Holy Toxic Sludge, Batman!
Butte

We've all heard the old saw about taking lemons and making lemonade, but it takes a mountain of moxie to turn a toxic pit of deadly mining waste into a tourist attraction.

Welcome to the Berkeley Pit.

Once an open-pit mine that produced copper, silver, and gold, the Berkeley Pit mine was closed in 1982 after yielding more than a billion tons of mostly copper-rich ore. Once mining operations ceased, the water pumps at the bottom of the 1,800-foot-deep, mile-long pit were removed, and the groundwater from surrounding aquifers found its own level, as water is famous for doing.

The water is extremely acidic (2.5 pH, roughly equivalent to vinegar), which presents a serious environmental problem. Making matters worse are all the dangerous chemicals laced through the water, including arsenic, cadmium, zinc, and sulfuric acid, as well as all kinds of heavy metal. And I don't mean Iron Maiden.

The poisonous pit gained national attention in 1995 when a flock of migrating snow geese made the unfortunate decision to land in

Geese check in, but they don't check out.

the water. They all died, and 342 carcasses were recovered. There was some dispute about the true cause of death, with the mine's owners arguing that the geese had gotten hold of some bad wheat.

The Berkeley Pit has become the Montana poster child for Superfund sites, and work is under way to achieve mitigation for the groundwater problems. Local organizers decided to capitalize on the curious nature of this massive mining leftover, and have constructed a scenic overlook, complete with a gift shop. For a couple of bucks, you can walk through the 200-foot tunnel to the overlook and gaze upon America's largest Superfund site. Actually, it's quite beautiful.

One can only guess whether the gift shop offers stuffed snow geese bearing the legend, "Honk If You Love Arsenic."

The Berkeley Pit Viewing Stand is located on Continental Drive in Butte. Call (800) 735-6814 to learn more.

More Hard Rock Than a Metallica Show

Butte

The next time some joker says you have a head like a rock, take him to a place where you can contrast and compare: the Montana Tech Mineral Museum.

Located on Montana Tech's picturesque hilltop campus, the Mineral Museum houses one of the finest collections of rocks and minerals in the world. Open year-round, it's also free.

Walk up the steps to the third floor of the museum building and peruse the thousands of unique and beautiful ore samples, many pulled from the ground beneath Butte. As soon as you walk through the door, you're faced with a monstrous geode the size of a garbage can. It's been sliced in half to show the brilliant purple crystals that line the inside.

You'll see all manner of colorful rocks, like malachite, azurite, stibnite and hematite, maybe even the ultra-rare haveyougotalite. There's Vivianite, fluorite, wulfenite, and manganite. There's also a white and grey rock called Jamesonite, which sounds like it may have been named by a rockhound who was blasted on Irish whiskey. If you're into crystals, be prepared to gape. There is a purple amethyst as big as a cantaloupe, and crystals of all colors are on display—tourmaline, aquamarine, and others found throughout the West. One monster specimen, the Big Daddy, is a smoky quartz that stands nearly as tall as a man. Well, maybe Danny Devito.

The variety of colors, sizes, and shapes of the rocks is truly amazing. Slip through the space between two display cases near the entrance and you'll find yourself in the darkened "Fluorescent Room." A variety of light-reactive rocks dazzle the eye under special ultraviolet and fluorescent lighting. Sorry, there are no Led Zeppelin posters.

There's even a petrified section of dinosaur spine that was found in the Hell Creek Formation near Jordan. Tell your joker friend that it's obviously a sacrum from an *Edmontosaurus*. Who's the hardhead now?

★ ★

The Mineral Museum is located in the museum building on the campus of Montana Tech in Butte. Dig deeper by calling (406) 496-4152 or visiting their Web site at www.mbmg.mtech.edu/museum/museum-exhibits.asp.

She's So Big, She Makes Even Non-Catholics Feel Guilty
Butte

When the people of Butte decide to honor an inspirational figure, they don't mess around. Witness the 90-foot-tall Our Lady of the Rockies, a likeness of Mother Mary perched atop the Continental Divide.

Putting her closer to town would have been the easy
way, but it wouldn't have been the cowboy way.

★ ★

Looming over the city, she gazes down from 8,510 feet above sea level and some 3,500 feet above Butte. With a beatific expression on her 10-foot-tall face, she holds her palms out to her sides, as if to say, "Are you going to fix that hole, or what?"

Our Lady of the Rockies began as the idea of Bob O'Bill (or was it Bill O'Bob?), who wanted to create a life-size statue to thank God for his wife's recovery from an illness. The idea grew into a community-wide movement, and after six years of work, the steel-skinned statue was airlifted in four sections onto the East Ridge by a Ch-54 Sikorsky Sky Crane helicopter from the Nevada Air National Guard. It must have been pretty surreal to watch the Sky Crane, looking like the

It's Like a Hug in a Pie Crust. With Gravy.

Of all the delicacies that Montana is known for, perhaps the most famous is the sturdy and filling, Butte-based meal in a crust, the mighty pasty.

It doesn't rhyme with "tasty," although it definitely is. It rhymes with "nasty," which it most definitely is not. The pasty is basically a meat and potato pie sealed in a pastry crust, kind of a cross between a pot pie and a calzone. Served smothered in steaming brown gravy with a side of coleslaw, this venerable dish has been around for a century or more.

Oh, sure, you can find a pasty in Missoula, say, or even Billings. But as any denizen of the Richest Hill on Earth will tell you, those things will be mere Pop-Tarts compared to the authentic Butte version.

Pasties were introduced to Butte by the Welsh and Cornish hard rock miners who came over from the Old Country. Working all day in the mines gave the men a powerful hunger, and when they opened their lunch boxes to find a hearty pasty or two, they'd say it was like

★ ★

giant offspring of a dragonfly and a grasshopper, lift the statue's head section into place. Thousands of Butte's fine citizenry watched and cheered from below.

The road leading up the mountain to the statue's base had to be blasted out of the rock; volunteers doing the work sometimes gained only 10 feet a day. Four hundred tons of concrete were poured for the base. Today, two-hour tours are given via bus rides up the mountain road.

The community of Butte raised funds for the project for years, paying for it entirely from donations and memorials. Our Lady of the Rockies provided a focus of pride for one of Montana's proudest,

finding "a letter from 'ome." With nowhere to wash the toxic filth off their hands before eating lunch, the men embraced the clever pasty. The thick edge of the half-round crust served as a handle, allowing the men to eat the pie without actually having to touch it with their fingers. Then they would throw the crusts down the mine as a token of bribery or appreciation for the underground spirits, or "knockers."

Pasties can be found filled with ground beef and potatoes, but the real McCoy, like the steaming specimens at Joe's Pasty Shop in Butte, use round steak. A few onions, some potatoes, and a little salt and pepper—nothing too mysterious about Butte's original comfort food. It will fill you up, for sure. In fact, I'm not so sure it's coincidental that one of Joe's pasties seems to be exactly the size and shape of a human stomach.

Joe's Pasty Shop is located at 1641 Grand Avenue in Butte.

They're open from 6 a.m. to 7 p.m., Monday through Friday, and from 6 a.m. to 6 p.m. on Saturday. Call (406) 723-9071 to learn more about their tasty, decidedly non-nasty treats.

most interesting cities at a point when their economy was shrinking due to troubled times in the extractive industries. Now this magnificent statue, dedicated to mothers and women everywhere, keeps a watchful eye over Butte, reminding its residents that, with faith and hard work, they are capable of great things.

Our Lady of the Rockies gift shop and information center is located at 3100 Harrison Avenue, #F1, in the Butte Plaza Mall. Call (800) 800-LADY or pay a visit to www.ourladyoftherockies.com.

Hey, We Can't Let the Irish Have *All* the Fun!
Butte

In Butte, St. Patrick's Day is to the Irish what the Force is to a Jedi Knight. It's Butte's defining essence, the biggest celebration of the year. Thousands of people converge from all corners of the country to swill Guinness, sing Celtic songs, and march through historic Old Butte in the big, drunken parade.

But for those of Finnish ancestry, St. Patrick's Day is just a day to sleep it off. The Finnish have their own patron saint, a man who is celebrated for driving the grasshoppers out of the vineyards of Finland, thus saving the wine, not to mention the jobs of all the vintners who produce it. That man was Saint Urho, and in Butte he's revered as the symbol of Finnish pride.

Saint Urho was actually a concoction of Richard Mattson of Virginia in 1956. He wanted a Finnish counterpart to St. Patrick. Some say Mattson chose the date of March 16 just to stick it to the Irish. Maybe so, but on March 16 of each year, the Finn community gathers at the Helsinki Yacht Club at the end of East Broadway (formerly the Corner Bar, the New Corner Bar, the Helsinki Bar, the Helsinki Bar and Grill, and the Helsinki Bar and Grill and Sauna. Seriously.). Dressed in purple-and-lime-green finery, the crowd packs into the bar and raise their glasses in celebration of Saint Urho, reveling in their heritage and the Finns' integral part in Butte's mining history. Indeed, it seems like the entirety of Finntown is packed into the Helsinki,

★ ★

where live music blares and the bartenders struggle to keep up with the thirsty throng. Kippis! ("Cheers!")

The party reaches a crescendo late in the afternoon when a new Saint and Princess are crowned. The Saint, a deserving Finn who may or may not be just off the boat, is properly feted and then draped in the lush purple cape and two-horned crown of Saint Urho. He is then presented with a pitchfork onto which is impaled a giant, stuffed grasshopper. The princess is similarly honored, but with a tiara and no farming implements. The new Saint then says a few words in his native Finnish, whipping the crowd into a frenzy, and vows to party until the wee hours.

St. Patrick's Day? If you're Finnish, that's for amateurs. Ilmatyyny-alukseni on täynnä ankeriaita! ("My hovercraft is full of eels!")

The Helsinki Yacht Club is located in Finntown, on East Broadway in Butte.

You mean this isn't normal?

On the Road Again, With Signs
Butte

Not far from the state prison in Deer Lodge where license plates
are made, there's a museum that collects them. Hundreds of them.
Thousands of them. Jeff Francis, owner of Butte's Piccadilly Museum,
collects, displays, buys, and sells thousands of license plates from all
over the world.

The driver of this 1914 Model T school bus probably
had a hard time getting the kids to keep their
heads and arms inside the windows.

★ ★

But this funky museum in Uptown Butte is more than just license plates. Oh, so much more. The main theme seems to be advertising and signs from American highway travel, but there are several tangents shooting off in all directions. Francis, an inveterate collector since age fourteen, has packed the Piccadilly with cherry vintage vehicles, gas station memorabilia, and road signs from all over the place.

There's a fabulous 1929 Ford Model A "Woody" Wagon that will make any car enthusiast drool into his toolbox. Parked next to it is an even more intriguing vehicle, a fully restored Model T school bus. There's even a flawless, sky blue specimen of the notorious 1959 Edsel, right around the corner from a shiny, 1939 Model 9N Ford tractor.

Vintage advertising signs cover the walls, ranging from a cheery Hancock's beer ad to a Raleigh bicycle sign that shows a young black man pedaling furiously, being chased by a ferocious lion. Kinda weird.

A beautiful Ford Model T station wagon is parked at a fully outfitted, old Mobil service station, both from an era when you could fill up your tank for the change that was in your pocket.

The Piccadilly also highlights other areas of early "modern" technology, from old television sets and radios to a staple of the Montana museum, the dentist's chair and its accompanying tools of torture.

You don't have to be a car nut to enjoy the Piccadilly, but if you are you'll be overwhelmed by the amount of stuff that is just plain cool. There are the hundreds of license plates and road signs on display, of course, but where else are you going to find the passenger-side door of the 1972 Indy 500 pace car? Presumably, it was blown off by Bobby Unser on his way to the checkered flag.

The Piccadilly Museum is located at 20 West Broadway Street. Open June through September, depending on weather, they can be reached by phone at (406) 723-3034, or on the Web at www.piccadilly museum.com.

★ ★

In Butte, He Was Man's Best (and Smelliest) Friend
Butte

You'd think that Montana's largest Superfund site might not be the healthiest place to keep a pet. But no one ever told that to the Auditor, a shaggy mutt who made the Berkeley Pit mine his home for seventeen years.

The Auditor—so named because he'd show up when you least expected it—was a skittish, reclusive dog that somehow survived for years while living in proximity to the acidic crust of this toxic mine. He was afraid of human contact, but was adopted by the miners as the

The bronze statue smells a lot better than the real thing.

★ ★

Trivia

Half of Montana's forest fires are caused by lightning. Forty-nine percent are human-caused. The remaining 1 percent are started by humans who have been hit by lightning.

de facto mascot for the Montana Resources mine. The men would leave food and water at the ramshackle doghouse they'd built for the pooch at the base of a huge waste rock dump.

"God only knows what he does all day," said mine employee Ron Benton in a 2002 edition of *The High Country News*. The Auditor looked like a cross between a used dust mop and Bob Marley, with his ratty, filthy ropes of hair covering his entire body, nearly dragging on the ground. The only appendage you could see was a hardened snout protruding from the doggie dreadlocks. Only once was a human able to approach him, when a miner actually trimmed his hair around his face. It is believed he was a Puli, a Hungarian breed of dog that has long, corded hair, and presumably smokes a lot of ganja.

The legend of the Auditor grew, even if he was only rarely captured in a photograph. He was regarded as the perfect symbol for Butte, a hard-knuckle town known for its toughness and resilience. When the Auditor died in 2003, local supporter Holly Peterson formed the Auditor Foundation, a nonprofit organization whose sole mission is to immortalize the dog through art and education. A statue of Butte's most famous dog can be seen at the Butte Plaza Mall. And the statue, unlike the dog, won't run away when you approach it.

The bronze statue of the Auditor is in the main concourse of the Butte Plaza Mall, 3100 Harrison Avenue.

★ ★

A Collection of Toys Older Than Some States

Deer Lodge

"You kids these days, you don't know how good you have it with your Nintendos, your iPods, your online video games, your robot dogs. You know what we had to play with when I was a kid? A tin can!"

The next time some sorehead geezer throws that diatribe your way, take him to Yesterday's Playthings in Deer Lodge. Across the street from the Old Prison, Yesterday's Playthings is Montana's finest museum of children's vintage toys and dolls.

"Ladies, we've got to do something about the proliferation of G.I. Joes!"

★ ★

Hundreds of dolls of all shapes and sizes comprise the bulk of the collection, most of them donated by Harriet Free. There are porcelain dolls, Shirley Temple dolls, and delicately crafted specimens as tall as 3 feet, some dating back to 1835. There is also a large display of teddy bears and a display cabinet groaning under the weight of hundreds of pieces of tea party china.

Also on display are several carriages and prams. One beautiful vintage stroller is crafted of basket weave and iron, and features an elaborate push handle that incorporates a built-in umbrella.

But it's not all about the dolls, by any means. The brick building, which once housed the prison's deputy warden as well as serving as the prison commissary, also contains dozens of pristine toy tractors and trucks. The Tonka display features several metal construction vehicles, reminding us that toys were once sturdy, American-made treasures that didn't break by the time Christmas vacation was over.

Model planes hang from the ceiling, including a four-engine bomber with a wingspan of more than 6 feet. There are also a few vintage pedal cars, restored to their original beauty. A bright red Allis-Chambers pedal tractor, complete with matching trailer, seems to be waiting to deliver a load of hay to some hungry cattle out on the ranch.

Once you see this amazing collection of toys and games from yesteryear, you'll begin to understand what Grandpa is ranting about. But if he claims that the only toys he had were a popsicle stick and an imaginary friend, it might be time to check his medication.

Yesterday's Playthings is on Main Street in Deer Lodge, across the street from the Old Prison Museum. Their phone number is (406) 846-1480.

What? No Batmobile?
Deer Lodge

The automobile. We may not have invented it, but it has become such an integrated part of our society that we've made its ascension into an American love story. Post-war economic boom. Western expansion. Solution to a million midlife crises. In America, especially out West, we love our cars.

And if you want to see them all together in one place, my friend, you have just found your nirvana. The Montana Auto Museum in Deer Lodge is home to over 120 cars and trucks (and a few weird contraptions that defy categorization). From a sparkling replica of the very first car (an 1886 Benz) to a pristine 1972 Dodge Charger, you can spend half a day eyeballing, admiring, and salivating over a warehouse full of beautifully restored examples of American technology in all its full, rubber-burning glory.

The vehicles are arranged in chronological order, artfully posed but off-limits to touching. You'll see a gleaming 1913 Cadillac set cheek-by-jowl to a 1915 Ford Model T. There are several delivery trucks, including a fabulous 1928 REO Speedwagon (no word on whether it was used for hauling soft rock).

The collection grew even larger when it recently acquired the Towe Ford Museum, which was liquidated by the IRS. You know what they say—when times are tough, your antique car collection is the first to go.

An old gas station office sits in one corner, looking like Goober just stepped out for an RC Cola. The walls of the museum are adorned with dozens of posters and ads, including a replica of a billboard from the mid-twentieth century. It features a winded greyhound, tongue hanging out, while a Ford roadster pulls away in the distance. "It's no use, Mac," reads the headline. "It's a Ford V-8."

It's hard to escape the retro vibe at this fascinating museum. Design enthusiasts can stroll through the decades and watch as America's design tastes display themselves in the cars' lines and overall styles. The fins of the 1950s are on full display, culminating in the glorious appendages at the rear of a 1959 Cadillac, ending a full 3 feet from the floor.

There is, of course, a generous gift shop at the end of your self-guided tour. It's easy to find. Just follow the Burma-Shave signs.

The Montana Auto Museum is located at 1106 Main Street, adjacent to the Old Prison Museum. Call (406) 846-3111 to learn more.

A 12-Foot Spike? I Wonder Where They Keep the Hammer

Deer Lodge

The last spike in the Milwaukee Road's coast extension was driven May 19, 1909, near Gold Creek, about 17 miles northwest of Deer Lodge. But who ever goes to Gold Creek? Thankfully, those in charge were savvy enough to build the Last Spike Monument in Deer Lodge, right along I-90.

Oh sure, there's the Golden Spike Monument at Promontory Summit, Utah, but is there anywhere nearby where you can get a

No, silly, it's not real gold.

★ ★

Montana-bred steak so big it hangs off the edges of your plate, like at the nearby Broken Arrow steakhouse? No, there is not.

The Last Spike Monument features an impossible-to-miss, 12-foot-tall railroad spike. It is not solid gold. In fact, I suspect Krylon spray paint played a role when the monument was dedicated on this site in 2003. It's still impressive, though, and makes for some great photo opportunities. There's also an informational plaque that tells you what all the fuss is about.

Also of interest is the double-ended train engine parked at the site. It is one of only twenty that were made in 1946 by General Electric for export to the Soviet Union. The electric engines, dubbed "Little Joes" because they were ordered by Joseph Stalin, were never delivered (thanks a lot, Cold War), and the Milwaukee Road could not put the engines into use themselves because they were designed to run on Russia's broad gauge rail. Oh, and all the controls were labeled in Russian.

The railroad company eventually did buy most of the engines after the Korean War, refitting them to run on American standard gauge rail. All in all, the Little Joe project was a money pit, and the last one stands near the giant Golden Spike, a testament to the vagaries of international wartime commerce.

The Last Spike Monument is accessible year-round, and is located on Main Street in Deer Lodge, at the end of the Old Prison Museum Complex. There is no charge for admission.

A Slice of Pioneer Life, Minus the Hardship
Deer Lodge

Imagine pulling a settler's wagon through the Pintler Range in the 1860s. At the end of the day, you dread the prospect of another meal of buffalo stew and soda bread, your kids have some kind of intestinal parasite, and you haven't seen a rest stop since St. Louis. Suddenly Deer Lodge is looking pretty good. That might have been the beginning of Cottonwood City.

"Which enclosure is it going to be?
Your choice, Mr. Convict."

★ ★

One hundred and fifty years later, Montana travelers can now stroll the boardwalk through Cottonwood City (or a facsimile thereof), the first Deer Lodge settlement. Several buildings have been meticulously restored to period specifications, and it doesn't take much imagination to get an idea of what pioneer life was like in the Wild West.

Located in Deer Lodge's historic Old Prison Museum Complex, Cottonwood City consists of nine buildings, including a schoolhouse, a church, a jail, post office, and two prairie cabins. The schoolhouse and one of the cabins are open to allow visitors to walk through and get a closer look at the trappings of pioneer life.

The Blood Cabin was restored by a trio of sisters: Mamie Swenson, Luella Tavenner, and Anita Sparks. Frontier Montana Museum staff provided guidance to ensure that the details were period-correct. Some of these details were family artifacts from the sisters' grand-parents who homesteaded near Avon in the late 1800s. It's not the original cabin, but its authenticity reflects the era nicely.

You can peer through the windows of the post office and witness a tableau straight out of the 1800s. A mannequin sits in a bathtub beneath a sign that advertises "25¢ Hot Baths." A large desk holds a log book, a vintage pair of eyeglasses (curiously, one lens is broken), and a telegraph key, giving the impression that the postmaster has just stepped away. There's also a barber/dentist chair that seems to be awaiting its next customer, a gentleman who might require the removal of either a beard or an abscessed molar.

There's no charge to prowl through Cottonwood City, and it's a fun way to spend an hour or so checking out the details of early Montana settler life and seeing how the pioneers unwound after a hard day of western expansion.

Cottonwood City is on Main Street in Deer Lodge, across the street from the Old Prison.

★ ★

This Museum Is Guaranteed to Make You Thirsty
Deer Lodge

Tucked in the back of Deer Lodge's Frontier Montana Museum is a blast from Montana's past as potent as any double shot of rotgut rye. Desert John's Saloon is a fabulous re-creation of an Old West watering hole, stuffed with enough artifacts and antique saloon gewgaws to keep any history-loving whiskey enthusiast enthralled for hours.

As you walk through the swinging doors, a voice booms out, welcoming you to Desert John's. It's John himself, or rather, an

"Sure, we serve crabs here. We serve anybody!"

★ ★

animatronic replica standing behind the bar, whiskey bottle at the ready. The motion-activated figure explains that the intricate, fully restored back bar came up the Missouri River on a steamboat from St. Louis. But like any astute drink slinger, John knows his customers are more interested in women than in history. "If you're looking for entertainment," he adds with a chuckle, "it'll be down in a while."

Thankfully, there are no animatronic floozies. But the bar is impressively outfitted, with several poker games seemingly under-way on the tables. There's an exquisite pool table built in 1909 and donated by Rus and Marie Ellsworth in 1990. Large photos show men standing at the bar over a century ago, proudly raising their whiskey glasses. The walls are covered with dozens of signs, trays, posters, and calendars, all advertising various brands of whiskey. In case you haven't noticed, whiskey seems to be the official obnoxicant of the Old West.

Walk past the bar into the back room and you'll encounter a collection of whiskey bottles so massive that it looks like something from Hunter S. Thompson's basement. The collection was donated by Marge Bloomquist, whose husband spent a large portion of his life collecting the hundreds of bottles. Some rare specimens are made of milk glass, an opaque white material. There are jugs, filigreed silver decanters, and a few massive, promotional bottles over 2 feet tall.

If you're visiting the Old Prison Complex in Deer Lodge, sidle in to Desert John's Saloon and let yourself be transported to the Old West. Just don't belly up to the bar and order an appletini. The saloon is inside the Frontier Montana Museum on 1107 Main Street in Deer Lodge. Try calling (406) 846-0026 to take a shot of yesteryear.

Caged Heat and Turkey Pete
Deer Lodge

Unless you've watched *Escape From Alcatraz* about fifty times, you'll never get the true feeling of doing time in a real, vintage penitentiary without visiting the Old Montana Prison in Deer Lodge. A visit is even better than the movie, really, because there's no sadistic jerk like Patrick McGoohan making your life miserable.

The self-guided tour takes about an hour, and for most people that's plenty of time. The creepiness factor gets pretty high once you find yourself inside the main building and see where the worst of the West paid their debts to society. The original prison was built—using mostly convict labor—in 1871 as a way to deal with the outlaws who left a trail of destruction through the Montana Territory in the nineteenth century.

The original wall was made of wood (despite the inmates' suggestions to use straw) but was replaced in 1894 with a massive sandstone fortification that extended 4 feet underground. Many prisoners attempted to tunnel under it; none succeeded.

You'll see evidence of the riot of 1959 that left three men dead, including the deputy warden. One of the guard towers still bears the damage from a bazooka blast that was fired by the National Guard in an attempt to stun the rioting inmates. Eventually, the authorities were able to rescue twenty-three hostages.

You'll learn about Turkey Pete, a colorful convict who eventually went loony. A model prisoner serving a life sentence for murder, Pete got his nickname because of his job tending the prison's turkeys. He was a model prisoner, that is, until he decided to sell his entire flock for 25 cents a head without permission from the administration. By that time old Pete was pretty demented and was a sure candidate for the nearby puzzle factory in Warm Springs. The prison authorities took pity on him, and allowed him to continue receiving his phony "paychecks" that were made up by the prison print shop. Pete used these checks to "pay" all the prison's operating expenses. He also claimed to use his funny money to rescue Brazil's coffee crop and purchase alfalfa seed from Pancho Villa, among other things. When Turkey Pete died in 1967 at age eighty-nine, he was treated to the only funeral ever held within the prison walls.

Another highlight is the "prison life" exhibit, which is full of

★ ★

photos depicting everyday prison life through most of the twentieth century. There's even a photo of the prison band from the 1960s. As with most rock band publicity photos, no one is smiling. You can also view the tag plant in the hospital building where the auto license plate factory was located. Iron stamps and die machines stand quiet and unused, but it's easy to imagine the facility buzzing with industrious activity. A new, modern prison facility opened 4 miles west of town in 1979. Inmates at the new prison still design and produce

What we have here is a failure to communi . . . hey!
Where'd everybody go?

many of the state's license plates, such as the classic "IH8JAIL."

The Old Montana Prison is located at 1106 Main Street in Deer Lodge. Call (406) 846-3111 to talk to them about paying a voluntary visit to the big house.

The Old West, Sanitized for Your Protection
Deer Lodge

Some western museums in Montana offer a vast collection of dusty artifacts and information; others look like nothing more than a garage sale with a $2 entrance fee. But then there are some museums you walk into and say to yourself, "Whoa. These guys have funding."

The Frontier Montana Museum in Deer Lodge is just such a place. No junk, and large, glassed-in displays offer everything you might imagine from the settler days of the late 1800s, from weapons to clothing to Indian-crafted beadwork and ceremonial dress. The lighting is subdued, soft western cowboy music drifts from the ceiling speakers, and the whole museum just exudes class and quality.

In the center of the room is a full-size cowboy camp, complete with a fully outfitted chuck wagon and blazing campfire. Okay, it's not a real fire, but strips of colored cloth do dance in the breeze of a hidden electric fan; I suppose you could use it to fry up a picture of a steak. It's hard to look at this tableau and not think of the baked bean scene from *Blazing Saddles*. Phew!

Another complete vignette is just inside the front doors, but you have to view it through a jail cell's barred door. Appropriately, it's a lawman's office complete with desk and safe. Assorted law-enforcement items are strewn artfully around to give the appearance that Johnny Law just stepped out to get a shave, or perhaps quaff a sarsaparilla.

A battery of restored firearms are on display, and you could spend hours poring over the hundreds of pistols, rifles, derringers, and flintlocks laid out for your inspection. One case holds an interesting collection of stuff called, "The Gambler's Essentials." Dice, chips, cards, a flask, a Bowie knife, and several samples of currency paint a vivid picture of the saloon cardsharp.

There's also an interesting display of law-enforcement equipment that would suggest there was no coddling of suspects in the Wild West. In addition to the aforementioned revolvers and rifles, there are handcuffs, leg irons, shackles, nightsticks, brass knuckles, and assorted knives. Makes you kind of wonder how today's peace officers are supposed to keep order with pepper spray and a Taser.

The Frontier Montana Museum is part of Deer Lodge's Old Prison Museum Complex on 1106 Main Street. Call (406) 846-3111 or mosey on down to www.pcmaf.org.

When Art Imitates Life
Dillon

When your throat is parched and you slide into the rustic Moose Bar in downtown Dillon some afternoon, it will take your eyes a few moments to adjust to the dim light. Situated in one of the original brick buildings that were built in the town's heyday, the Moose is a typical western watering hole full of friendly locals, a generous pour, and a great jukebox.

But as your vision becomes accustomed to the lower light, you'll see what appears to be a giant comic strip along the wall opposite the bar. It's a huge, colorful slice of bar life painted by local artist Bill Ferguson in 1964.

The style is straight out of the 1940s comic strips, more Barney Google than Mary Worth. One of the Moose's regulars, a gentleman named Carl, patiently walked me along the 20-foot-long mural. Carl's an old-timer who grew up in Dillon and so could name every character depicted in the rollicking cartoon. He even remembered Itchy, the smallest of several dogs in the scene (it probably helped that the word "ITCHY" was lettered on the dog's side).

The people in the mural are fighting, drinking, singing, hustling women, shooting craps, and otherwise just carousing and enjoying

Just another Saturday night in Dillon.

themselves on a typically rowdy night at the Moose Bar.

As I thanked Carl and headed for the jukebox to play some Hank Snow for him, I stepped around a couple of ranch dogs lying on the floor. I looked around at the other bar patrons and thought, wow, nothing's changed.

The Moose Bar is located at 6 North Montana Street in Dillon. Their phone number is (406) 683-4236.

★ ★

An Elephant Never Forgets . . . to Duck!
Dillon

Show business is littered with stories of celebrities who flamed out young, living a fast life only to be snuffed out at their peak by some tragic misfortune. A few obvious ones who come to mind are Kurt Cobain, James Dean, John Belushi, and Natalie Wood. And of course, Pitt the elephant.

Okay, so Pitt wasn't world-famous. And she wasn't exactly cut down in her prime. She was, after all, 102 years old. That's getting up there, even for an elephant. But when she performed with John Robinson's Military Elephants she was one of the most famous elephants of her time. And she died in spectacular fashion, getting struck by lighting during a circus performance with the Cole Brothers in 1943 at the Beaverhead County Fairgrounds in Dillon.

She was a tough old bird, er, elephant, having survived for years performing for another show, Robinson's Great Combination Show. But a 1916 bank panic caused Robinson to sell off most of his herd of pachyderms, at the time the largest in the world. He kept Pitt and three others on his farm in Terrace Park, Ohio, where he retired. Neighbors became used to the sight of elephants pulling plows and wandering around the dirt roads through the countryside.

After Robinson's death in 1942, his widow gave Pitt to the Cole Brothers Circus. Their troupe traveled around the country, and were performing in Dillon one night when a thunderstorm rolled into the area. The elephants huddled together and, with a clap of thunder and a flash of lightning, Pitt fell dead. She was killed instantly.

She was buried with a somber funeral ceremony, and circus folk placed hundreds of flowers at her grave. Eventually a wooden fence, roughly elephant-size, was erected around the gravesite. A granite marker is also in place, embedded at the foot of a young shade tree on the spot of the deceased circus star. The marker reads, "PITT – Killed on this spot by lightning Aug. 6, 1943 while showing with Cole

★ ★

Bros. Circus. Last of the John Robinson herd of Military Elephants. May God bless her."

Hopefully she's up there somewhere, in celebrity elephant heaven, eating out of a bottomless bowl of peanuts and not worrying about her weight.

The grave of Old Pitt is located at the Beaverhead County Fairgrounds in Dillon.

Beaverhead County Museum: It's For the Birds
Dillon

Dillon's Beaverhead County Museum is a multifaceted attraction that can easily hold a traveler's interest for half a day. The aggregation of buildings includes the main museum, built in the style of a pioneer cabin, and the original Dillon train depot, which houses one of the finest collections of Montana birds you'll see anywhere.

As you enter the main museum building, you're greeted by a snarling, 8-foot-tall Kodiak bear. The 1,200-pound bruin glares down at you as if you're the one who plugged him. Beyond the bear are myriad displays holding all sorts of items from the previous century and a half. Some are a bit older, however, like the woolly mammoth fossils that were found in the area.

The frontier collection fills two large rooms with objects from the pioneer era up to the early twentieth century. One photo accompanies the remarkable story of King Pharaoh, a 190-pound Great Dane who served as the Hotel Andrus's most interesting "bellboy." Seems Pharaoh was in the habit of carrying visitors' bags from the train station to the hotel two blocks away. Occasionally he would also grab the suitcases of guests of the Melton Hotel and carry them to the Andrus.

All kinds of nineteenth-century clothing, tools, and everyday items are here for your perusal. One display celebrates J. Fred Woodside, Dillon's first pilot. But it's airborne creatures of another species that prove the most fascinating of all.

If you ask them nicely, these birds will hold
real still while you take a photo.

The roomful of mounted, native Montana birds in the depot will
take your breath away. More than one hundred birds, from the smallest titmouse to Louis the snow goose, are expertly displayed. A pair
of crows seems to be picking away at a split bag of corn while spar-
rows bring sticks and shreds of tree bark to their nest. Above the displays, a couple of raccoons lounge patiently, as if waiting for a bird
to abandon her nest of eggs.

Be sure you've got plenty of time when you visit the Beaverhead
County Museum. The Dillon area has a rich history, and the museum
does a fine job of covering it all. It's located at the Union Pacific
Depot in downtown Dillon.

★ ★

In Ennis, They're Big Into Fly Fishing
Ennis

When someone talks about a guy who's a "big fly fisherman," he just may be referring to the biggest fly fisherman of them all.

This titan of trout fishing stands on a triangle of grass where US 287 meets East Main Street in Ennis. Crafted of sheet metal and iron, the 10-foot-tall fly fisherman seems to be knee-deep in a stream,

Motorists, do not be alarmed. Just don't let
this guy catch you using a worm.

★ ★

tangling with a trophy trout on the other end of his line. The sculpture is the work of Jim Dolan, a well-known artist based in Belgrade. His wildlife sculptures can be seen throughout the state. Some of his pieces, like this giant fly fisherman, are quite whimsical indeed.

According to a plaque at the base of the fisherman, the sculpture

From the Lower Forty to the Front Nine

In the rich farmland between Dillon and Twin Bridges, miles of sprinkler pipe irrigate thousands of acres of crops. Farm machinery hums from sunup to sundown, and the hardy souls who work the land put their entire beings into each day, sweating with the honest, rewarding labor of the farmer and rancher. At the end of the day, when it's time to wind down and perhaps reward oneself with a bit of leisure or a cold brew, well, there's only one place to go.

You head over to Phil Taylor's place to play nine holes of golf.

Phil is a developer and land baron who loves to build things. I asked him what, exactly, motivated him to build his own golf course. "Stupidity," he says with a laugh.

He's played the game since he was twelve, but his adult life has been spent as a dry-land farmer and a developer who's built two or three subdivisions. "I always liked playing with backhoes, dozers, graders, and loaders," he says. The golf course idea came to him when he sold off all but the wet bottom area of several hundred acres. He was digging around with an excavator one day when he wondered if he could make a golf hole on that spot.

★ ★

was donated by William J. (Nick) and Gail Simmons of Big Canoe, Georgia, and McAllister, Montana. It's a fitting piece for this fish-crazy town on the banks of the famous Madison River.

The detail in the Brobdingnagian back caster is worth a closer look, and some of the materials used in the construction are pretty

His daydream expanded, he says, and he began imagining a fair-way here, a tee box there, and before he knew it, he was constructing a regulation, nine-hole course. The water to manage the course, however, became prohibitively expensive, so he shortened the length to that of an executive course, featuring a couple of par fours and the rest par threes.

Sleepy Hollow, as he's named it, was completed and opened to the public in 2005. The graceful curves and verdant fairways rival most municipal courses for physical beauty and sheer playability. He had a couple of golf course experts from Billings help him execute the final stages, like shaping the greens and such, to make sure everything was, ah, up to par.

He's planning on a tenth hole, which will feature a turn-of-the-century cabin that currently sits on its original site near his shop. He wants to clean out the cabin and move it to provide golfers with a shelter from the rain.

As he sits astride one of his tractors, absently flicking levers and knobs while he tells his story, I have no doubt that we'll be looking at eighteen holes before you know it.

Sleepy Hollow Golf Course is located at 600 Tory Drive, just north of Dillon. Call (406) 683-6118 for directions.

★ ★

clever, too. The fly line, for instance, is a long strand of steel cable. Of course, if you're fly casting with steel cable, you'd better be 10 feet tall and bulletproof, like this guy.

Dolan's *Madison Valley Angler* is located at the intersection of US 287 and East Main Street in Ennis.

See It for Yourself: The Rocky Mountain Hyena
Ennis

Until someone captures or kills a bigfoot, most of us will remain skeptical of the existence of the Sasquatch, the yeti, the abominable snowman, or any other iteration of the large, hairy, smelly creature of legend.

But here in Montana we've got an actual specimen of a frightening mythical creature. Maybe it's not a bigfoot but it's scary enough. Known by such names as the Creature, the Madison Valley Monster, and Shunka Warak'in (as he was called by Native Americans), this legendary beast continues to terrorize livestock and scare the bejesus out of ranchers throughout the Northwest. Meet the Rocky Mountain hyena.

As the story goes, Madison Valley rancher I. A. Hutchins shot the animal in 1886 when he saw it on his land. He'd been losing sheep to a predator, and at night he could hear unearthly screams coming from the sheep pen. The sounds made his hair stand on end. In the process of killing the beast, though, he accidentally shot one of his cows. So he traded the mystery creature's lifeless carcass to Joseph Sherwood for a new cow.

Sherwood, a taxidermist, was unable to identify the animal. Neither could anyone else. A detailed description was sent to the Smithsonian, but they were baffled. It looks wolf-like, but instead of the grey/tan/black colors normally seen on wolves, this animal's coat is mostly yellow and red, with faint stripes down its sides. The snout is much narrower than a wolf's, and its sloping back and shoulders give it more the look of a hyena. Sherwood put the mount on display at

No flash photography allowed, but even with the glare
you can still see how scary this fellow is.

his store-museum in Henry's Lake, Idaho, and for years the creature
fueled speculation that the ongoing sheep slaughters in the area
were being carried out by these strange, wolf-like beasts.

After being hidden away for decades upon the sale of the Henry's
Lake store, the creature resurfaced in the Natural History building at
Idaho State University in Pocatello. It is now on loan to the Madison
Valley History Museum in Ennis. You can go see for yourself what
this mystery creature looks like. Just don't wear a sheepskin coat; you
might be pushing your luck.

★ ★

The Madison Valley History Association Museum is just south of the Town Pump store on the west end of Main Street. Admission is free, although donations are accepted. They open in May on Memorial Day weekend and remain open until the end of September. Their hours are 10 a.m. to 4 p.m., Tuesday through Sunday. Their Web site is http://madisonvalleyhistoryassociation.org.

Whole Lotta Shakin' Goin' On
Ennis and West Yellowstone

When you're camping with your family in one of the hundreds of picturesque campgrounds in this magnificent state, there are a few things you probably need to worry about: mosquitoes, sunburn, bears, the occasional prowling cougar, and how to get the kids to eat something other than Vienna sausages. One thing that doesn't normally fit into this list of dangers is the possibility of an entire mountainside being shaken loose and burying the campground.

That's exactly what happened on August 17, 1959, when the most powerful earthquake ever recorded in the Rocky Mountains struck the Hebgen Lake area. A huge rockslide rumbled down the mountainside above a Madison River Canyon Gorge campground, burying the site and killing nineteen people instantly. Others were swept away in the river or struck by falling trees. All told, twenty-eight people lost their lives in the disaster.

More than one hundred others were trapped as the landslide and resulting flood cut off any escape. Shivering, terrified survivors huddled together under the full moon all night, and were finally rescued when Air Force helicopters and Forest Service smokejumpers arrived on the scene at dawn.

In Yellowstone Park 200 geysers blew their stacks. Two-lane highways were cracked and broken into pieces like Oreo cookies. The temblor, the fourth strongest ever in the U.S. up to that point (it measured 7.5 on the Richter scale), was felt in eight states across an area of 500,000 square miles.

The massive rockslide plugged up the Madison River, forming what is known today as Quake Lake. Fifty years later only a few hundred pines have grown back in the devastated area of the mountain. The immense, jagged rockslide is still there, plain as day, a reminder of that horrifying night when Mother Nature snapped her fingers and changed the landscape of the valley, as well as hundreds of lives. There's an excellent Forest Service visitor center that tells the story of the earthquake in words and pictures, as well as a very informative short video. Vienna sausages not included.

The Earthquake Lake Visitor Center is between Ennis and West Yellowstone. Their Web site is www.visitmt.com/categories/more info.asp?IDRRecordID=9546&SiteID=1.

What's Next—Sky Snorkeling?
Georgetown Lake

Falling firmly into the esteemed Montana category of "How Else Can We Get Through This Long Friggin' Winter," the new thrill sport of snowkiting combines snowboarding and skiing with windsurfing, and tosses in elements of parasailing as well. Winter-loving thrill seekers have invented a sport that is, um, snowballing in popularity with each ski season.

High in the Pintler Mountains between Philipsburg and Anaconda, you'll find Georgetown Lake, a favorite year-round fishing spot for generations of Montanans. The lake is teeming with trophy rainbow trout, huge brookies, and, in the winter, delicate silver salmon. For the past few years, however, Georgetown has also served as the site of the annual Montana Snowkite Rodeo, held in mid-February.

Ice fishing shanties dot the lake. If it's a sunny day, most fishermen sit outside on upturned five-gallon buckets, patiently jigging with foot-long fishing rods. The kiters, by contrast, zip around the lake like stones skipping across water, harnessing the wind with their high-tech, U-shaped kites. The two groups coexist, though, and while

✦ ✦

a kiter/ice shack collision would be spectacular and very entertaining, it's exceedingly rare.

Georgetown Lake is well known for its consistent, strong winds, and the lake's broad expanse and easy highway access make it perfect for kiteboarding. And while kiters enjoy carving in the

Ski hill? We don't need no stinking ski hill.

★ ★

backcountry, doing tricks in terrain parks, and cruising through mountain meadows, at Georgetown Lake it's all about the need for speed. This is the Bonneville Salt Flats for the wind-driven sliders, and speeds

They Got Frostbite Just Thinking About It

You think it got a little chilly last night in your camper at the RV park? Chances are it wasn't so cold that your face would freeze into a solid mask in the few seconds it takes to go outside and check the propane tank. Unless, that is, you happened to be camping at Rogers Pass, and it was January 20, 1954.

At a miner's camp near the crest of the Continental Divide, the temperature dropped to 70 degrees below zero, the coldest temperature ever recorded in the lower forty-eight. All picnics were cancelled. There were gunfights over a pair of long johns. Rather than venture out to the latrine and have sensitive body parts turned into ice cubes, miners decided to hold it.

But that was positively balmy compared to the *world's* coldest temperature ever recorded. On July 21, 1983, at a Russian research station in Vostok, Antarctica, the mercury dropped to minus 128.6. And that's not even including the wind chill. You can bet they were all wearing those awesome Russian fur hats.

The spot in Montana is marked by a small informational sign. It makes for a good photo opportunity; later, when the chips are down and your spouse is complaining about the cold, you can whip out the photo and say, "Look, honey, it could be worse."

Rogers Pass is about 30 miles northeast of Lincoln on MT 200.

of 45 to 50 miles per hour can have the poor ice fishermen shaking in their Klondikes. Huge jumps are built out of snow, and kiters perform tricks and stunts, always at the mercy of the capricious mountain winds.

When kiters gather for their annual rodeo in February, the sky over the lake is dotted with dozens of brightly colored nylon kites. It's Montana's equivalent of Albuquerque's hot air balloon festival. But at Georgetown Lake the hot air is replaced by adrenaline.

Georgetown Lake is located between Philipsburg and Anaconda on the Pintler Scenic Route, MT 1. Visit www.montanakitesports.com for more information.

Above Here There Be Dragons
Helena

If you're walking along Helena's charming pedestrian mall near Last Chance Gulch, don't forget to look up. On top of the Atlas Block where the Upper Missouri Artists Gallery is located on the ground floor, you can see a trio of bright green dragons coiled around the stubby minaret on the building's roof.

Well, they're not dragons, actually. According to the historical marker on the front of the building, they're salamanders, a much less fearsome creature. But with a fresh coat of green paint and their batlike wings extended as they seem to crawl around the minaret, they don't look like any salamander you might have found in the pond when you were a kid.

The Atlas Block is one of the buildings constructed by suddenly rich miners during Helena's gold rush of the 1880s. This one was built in 1889 by the S. J. Jones Insurance Company in the Richardsonian Romanesque architectural style. Helena architects Fisk J. Shaffer and James F. Stranahan designed the building.

After 118 years the dragons (or salamanders, or gargoyles) were almost unrecognizable from weathering, so they were removed, repaired, and given a fresh coat of lizard green paint. They now cling proudly to the spire at the top of the building, looking almost lifelike as they curl and twist around the minaret.

The Atlas Block is located at 7-9 North Last Chance Gulch in Helena. You can see the dragons from Park Avenue and beyond.

This looks like an outtake from *Ghostbusters*.

★ ★

The Edgar Winter of the Bison World

Helena

When Ted Nugent recorded "The Great White Buffalo" with the
Amboy Dukes back in the 1970s, he exposed a whole generation of
white rock and roll fans to a Native American ideal, to a mystical beast
revered by the Plains Indians as a harbinger of future events. Oua Oia,
his Indian name, is still a sacred spirit that endures in Indian culture.

You can see Montana's most famous white buffalo for yourself at
the Montana Historical Society Museum in Helena, across the street
from the capitol building. The white buffalo mount on display, Big

"I just asked for some frosted tips—
I'll never go to that salon again."

Medicine, was born in Moiese in 1933. He lived there on the National Bison Range until his death in 1954. His popularity made him the most photographed buffalo in the world.

Not actually a true albino, Big Medicine (or "Whitey," as he was known by the Bison Range staff) has blue eyes (not pink) and a brown topknot of hair between his horns. He was mounted by Browning artist Bob Scriver, and holds a place of honor on the second floor of the museum overlooking the lobby.

The security guards are quick to tell visitors that no flash photography is allowed. "Don't use a flash or he'll come to life," they say, half-seriously. He's an impressive beast to be sure. He weighed as much as 1,900 pounds, was 6 feet tall at the hump, and measured 12 feet from nose to tail. That's a lot of buffalo.

This sacred animal was a powerful symbol to the Indian culture, and to some he still represents the pride and the perseverance of the Native American way of life. Nugent, the Motor City Madman, knew what they were talking about:

> Well, he got the battered herd. He led 'em cross the land.
> With the Great White Buffalo, they gonna make a final stand.

The Montana Historical Society Museum Library is located at 225 North Roberts Street in Helena. Their hours are Monday through Saturday from 9 a.m. to 5 p.m.; on Thursday evenings they're open until 8 p.m. Call (406) 444-2694 or visit www.his.state.mt.us/museum.

It Had to Be Bluestone—Yellowstone Was Already Taken
Helena

There are a lot of crazy-looking, pioneer-era structures still standing in Helena. From the collection of cabins on Reeder's Alley to the oddly shaped skyscrapers downtown, there's one house that stands alone— literally—among these historic buildings. It's the Bluestone House near Cruse Street, and its story is as hazy as the Helena air during fire season.

★ ★

Currently inhabited by the Meloy Law Firm, the Bluestone House sits on a hill overlooking Last Chance Gulch, the epicenter of Helena's historic gold rush days. Just up the hill from it is the original Last Chance Gulch fire lookout, which actually burned down several times. Seriously.

The Bluestone House gets its name from the bluish gray granite blocks used in its construction. The house was built either as a brothel, a castle, or a private home, depending on which legend you choose to believe. Its location in the middle of several houses of ill repute would suggest its function as a place miners would go to get their nuggets panned, if you get my drift. But other, more-substantiated assertions claim that the Bluestone House was built in 1905 by James Stranahan to be used as a private home. The title changed hands many times over the years, but the house was rarely occupied by any of its owners during its existence.

In 1935 the famous structure was badly damaged by an earthquake. In the 1970s, the house was reconstructed and refurbished using grant money from the Urban Renewal Historic Preservation Committee. Laborers painstakingly took the remaining house apart, inventorying and numbering each individual block of granite so it could be pieced back together properly. That's some major attention to detail. Nowadays, you're lucky if you can get a contractor to return a phone call. This was reportedly the most expensive historic restoration of any building in the U.S. up to that time.

The Bluestone House is located at 80 South Warren Street, and is visible from most of the Last Chance Gulch area.

How Can He Sleep Through That Pine Beetle Infestation?
Helena

If you look to the north while you're in Helena, you can see what looks like the shape of a man lying flat on his back and staring up at the Big Sky. Meet the Sleeping Giant. Keep your voice down, because you don't want to wake up this mountain-size fella.

★ ★

He looks a little like Alfred Hitchcock, don't you think?

His nose is actually a 600-foot rock that's a part of Beartooth Mountain. That should give you some idea of the scale of this dude. He's long been a landmark known by locals in the Capital City. Lewis and Clark stayed at the base of the Sleeping Giant in 1805 during their first journey to the Northwest, but they probably were unaware of the whimsical shape of the mountain.

When you're looking out across the forests at the Sleeping Giant, just be grateful that his silhouette doesn't include a strategically placed ponderosa pine. Talk about a woody.

The Sleeping Giant is visible (on relatively clear days) due north of Helena.

Sluice Box Heroes
Helena

The sluice box, or rocker box, was a popular method of separating gold from dirt and sand during the mining boom in Helena in the late 1880s. Adopted from the gold rushes of California and the Klondike, the sluice box was designed to use flowing water to flush raw material across a series of riffles, allowing the heavier gold dust and flakes to settle into the ridges where it could be more easily retrieved.

While panning by hand remains the most iconic method of searching for gold, the use of the more-efficient and higher-capacity sluice box was prevalent along the streams of Last Chance Gulch. To commemorate this method of gold recovery, a sculpture by prolific Billings artist Lyndon Fayne Pomeroy was erected in Helena's pedestrian mall in 1974.

Titled *Prospector Fountain,* it's a large installation with a life-size, three-level sluice box being operated by two stylized miners. The iron and steel sculpture is complete with running water, fed by a concrete "stream" that winds its way up through the mall. Water flows down through the sluice box, emptying into a cement pond surrounded by river rocks.

The sculpture of gold seekers stands right in front of the Montana State Fund building, which is either ironic or appropriate, depending on how you look at it.

The *Prospector Fountain* is in the pedestrian mall in Helena.

It's a Bird! It's a Plane! In the Street! It's a Train!
Helena

It's not the California Zephyr but it's not exactly a city bus either. It's Helena's Last Chance Tour Train, and there's no better way to cram a boxcar load of Helena's rich history into one hour.

For $7.50 a pop, the 95-foot-long train hauls about fifty tourists at a time through the streets of the Queen City. The "conductor"

★ ★

chatters nonstop about historic events, interesting architecture, famous people, and how much she loves her job. It's a whirlwind tour and, if you're unfamiliar with the city, you'll take so many twists and turns that by the time you get back to the starting point, you won't know which way is up.

The train passes by a few daycare centers, and the kids are always out in the summertime, waiting for it. The conductor blows her whistle and the kids scream and stamp their feet and yank on the chain link fence like chimpanzees at feeding time. Even the adults smile when the train goes by.

At one point the tour runs up the hill from the foot of Last Chance Gulch and past Reeder's Alley. The road gets pretty dicey there, and passengers in the last car actually leave their seats for a moment over the bigger bumps.

All aboard for a history-saturated tour of the Queen City!

The drivers all seem to possess way more knowledge about Helena than anyone will ever need, but that's really what you want in a tour guide, isn't it? One of the most interesting stories you might hear occurs as the train passes the ornate St. Helena Cathedral. The main features of the building are the twin spires that rise up hundreds of feet in the air. As the story goes, sometime early in the twentieth century, a pilot made a $100 bet that he could fly his plane between the spires. Someone took him up on it. After successfully making the flight, and according to the story, he measured his wingspan and discovered that he'd cleared the spires by 3 inches.

I wasn't able to find any corroboration to that story, but when it comes over the loudspeaker straight from the Last Chance Tour Train conductor, it just has to be true, right? All aboard!

The tour train departs from the Montana Historical Society, just east of the capitol building at the corner of Sixth and Roberts. Take a tour past their Web site at www.lctours.com.

This Miner's Cabin's a Two-fer
Helena

The Emil Kluge home in Helena is listed in the National Register of Historic Places, and under "Architectural Style," it says, "No Style Listed." Once you see the place, you'll know why.

For some reason, Kluge built a two-story house that's like two different kinds of houses grafted together in some contractor's worst Frankenstein nightmare. A prominent mason, Kluge came to Helena from Germany in 1873. In 1882 he moved his family into an abandoned miner's cabin. He salvaged bricks, timbers from an old flume, and other materials to construct the second story using a building technique he brought from the Old Country.

Kluge later became one of Helena's first police officers, and went on to serve as street commissioner and constable. He also served two terms as justice of the peace. He died in 1924.

By the mid-1960s the "Maverick House," as it's known locally, had degenerated into a decrepit haven for transients and reefer-loving kids. The city was on the verge of tearing it down, saying it was a fire hazard. Fortunately, the owner was located, the building was restored, and it was added to the National Register of Historic Places.

The Kluge House is currently occupied by a business, but you can drive right by and see the upside-down architecture that, to its credit, has stood for well over one hundred years. It's located at 540 Last Chance Gulch in Helena, and is included in the Last Chance Gulch train tour.

Her Only Crime Was Overacting
Helena

Wow, talk about crime and punishment. This building would make Papillon look like the Four Seasons by comparison. The Lewis and Clark County Jail, as it was called when it was built in 1890, is one imposing edifice of stone and iron.

These days, however, it is the home of the Myrna Loy Center for the Performing and Media Arts. Loy, the celebrated actress of the early "talkies" era, was a Helena native. But there are still bars on the windows, and the medieval look of the building strikes fear in the heart of anyone who has ever run afoul of The Man.

In the nineteenth century it was a popular attitude in architecture that a building's design should reflect its function. With that in mind, the jail was built in the Romanesque style, using local granite to achieve a somber effect. The Helena firm of Paulson and McConnel designed and built the jail, under contract with the Detroit Lock and Safe Company. It continued to serve as the county jail until the early 1980s.

One story about the jail is gleefully repeated by local tour guides: The county sheriff was so proud of his building that he actually hosted his daughter's wedding reception there. That seems kind of unlikely, unless (like most fathers of the bride) he was trying to save some coin on renting a hall.

While not really known as a haunted building, a few strange and mysterious events have been whispered about over the years. The downstairs area, particularly near the women's restroom, has recently been the site of some pretty heavy paranormal activity. Could it be the ghost of Myrna Loy herself, coming back to see where she left her car keys?

The Myrna Loy Center for the Performing and Media Arts is located at 15 North Ewing in Helena. Call (406) 443-0287 or visit www.myrnaloycenter.com.

The Newsboy Gets His Due
Helena

Watch where you're going on Helena's walking mall. If you have a collision with the Newsboy, you're going to lose. Sure, he's only about the size of an average ten-year-old, but he's made of bronze.

The lifelike sculpture, entitled *Extra, Extra*, was created and donated to the city by Becky Eiker in 1999. She and her husband, Bill, had established the Becky Eiker Foundation three years earlier, and the Newsboy, as it's known locally, was given to the city as a gesture of thanks to its citizens.

He holds aloft a newspaper in one hand, and several more are tucked under his other arm. In his early-twentieth-century garb of button-down shirt, suspenders, and a cloth hat, he seems to be calling out, offering up the latest edition of the daily news to anyone who passes by.

An inscription at the base of the sculpture spells it out: "Extra! Extra! Read all about it! A tribute to the faithful newsboys who sold their papers on these street corners, bringing the latest news to the people of Helena." In the dangerous, rough-and-tumble, gold rush days of Last Chance Gulch, this ten-year-old boy might have been considered middle-aged.

Extra, Extra is located at the end of the Last Chance Gulch walking mall, near the intersection of Sixth Avenue and Last Chance Gulch.

They're called newspapers. People used to
read them before the Internet.

Thurston Howell III Would Feel Right at Home

From the outside, it appears to be just another oddly shaped downtown brick building, and a rather frumpy one at that. But inside it was one of the more opulent buildings of gold rush–era Helena. The Montana Club in Helena was once home to the most exclusive club in Montana, maybe in the world.

During Helena's mining boom of the 1880s (the town was then known as Last Chance Gulch), there were more millionaires per capita in that city than anywhere in the world. These millionaires needed somewhere to congregate, a place where they could light each other's cigars with $100 bills and defunct mining deeds. That place was the Montana Club, formed in 1885, and the requirements for membership were simple: millionaires only.

Astonishingly, the club had as many as 134 members at one time. You can just imagine these gold-dusted fat cats getting together over dinner, feasting on Blue Point oysters, Russian caviar, roasted bald eagle, and diamond-encrusted king crab served in ivory saucers with melted polar bear butter. They'd enjoy thousand-year-old scotch after dinner, burping up dollar signs while they looked out the windows, gleefully dry-washing their hands over their extractive industry empire.

Today the Montana Club still exists as a thriving gathering spot for Helena's movers and shakers. The membership requirements have been somewhat relaxed: A $200 initiation fee gets you in, and the dues are about $70 a month.

The Montana Club is located at 24 West Sixth Avenue in Helena. Their phone number is (406) 442-5980, and they're on the Web at www.mtclub.org.

Weirdness in the Park

Helena

Is it a snake? Is it a landlocked sea serpent? Is it a group of alien pods emerging from the turf? Is it a family of giant nautilus shells playing hide and seek? The answer may lie in the title of this public artwork: *All Of the Above, None Of the Above.*

The group of pale green mystery creatures was created by artist Chip Clawson in 2007. He was awarded a commission to create a piece of public art for Pioneer Park, and came up with a circular installation of ceramic, vaguely crustacean-looking, donut-shaped objects that appear to be emerging from the ground. He

It's either some kind of giant snail dance or an extremely lost Flathead Monster.

★ ★

incorporated a couple of benches right into the design. You can sit there at your leisure and wonder what the heck you're looking at.

Pioneer Park is located just behind the library on Last Chance Gulch in Helena.

An Architectural Oddity
Helena

If you're driving down Last Chance Gulch in Helena, don't forget to look up. In a deeply historic city with lots of one-hundred-year-old buildings, it can be easy to overlook some of the more interesting details.

One such captivating feature is the corner of the Power Block

You gotta love an architect who does stuff just to see if you're paying attention.

building at the foot of the walking mall on Last Chance Gulch. If you look closely at the six-story, Romanesque-revival building, you'll see that each story has one more window on the corner than the one below it. It's a subtle architectural touch that reflects the imagination and creativity of Senator T. C. Power, who built the structure in 1888.

Power had other buildings throughout the city, many of which are still standing, including his original rose-quartz home that can be seen on the upper west side. But the Power Block is his most well-known building, still filled with offices and businesses more than a century after its construction.

The T. C. Power Block is at the intersection of Sixth Avenue and Last Chance Gulch in Helena.

Helena's Own Central Park, Without the Muggings
Helena

There are city parks and then there are City Parks. In Helena, they've turned an entire mountain into a CITY PARK.

Mt. Helena City Park is the largest city park in the state. In fact, the only larger one in the whole country is that little weed patch in Manhattan known as Central Park. But the two green spaces couldn't be more different.

Sprawling over 620 acres, the city park covers Mt. Helena. A trail system cobwebs its base and leads up to its peak, 5,468 feet above sea level. Helena residents and passers-through visit the area in droves, and there's ample parking at the entrance. The trails, leading through pine trees and low scrub, are dotted with benches and picnic tables.

At least six trails wind through the park, some leading past the giant letter H up to the peak and others connecting with trails that lead into the Helena National Forest. You can also hike to a cave known as the "Devil's Kitchen." (Note to city planners: You might get more traffic if you renamed it "Devil's Food Kitchen." Just sayin'.)

The views from Mt. Helena City Park are spectacular at any time of the year. The Montana air is generally pretty clear, allowing visibility

★ ★

to mountains more than 50 miles away. You can also see many of the Capital City's more famous landmarks, such as the spires of the St. Helena Cathedral, the seventeen-story minaret of the Civic Center, and the green-domed capitol building.

There's Nothing to See Here. Move It Along. Show's Over.

Montana seems to have more than its share of paranoid crackpots. From various survivalist movements to Garfield County's Freemen, it seems that Big Sky Country serves as a Last Best Hiding Place for reactionary fundamentalists with a burning desire to escape the oppression they feel they're suffering. From our lack of a posted speed limit on the interstates in the 1990s to the staunch opposition to a sales tax (even during government budget shortfalls), Montana personifies the rugged individuality of the Wild West mindset.

Perhaps the most notorious of all anti-establishment rabble-rousers was Ted Kaczynski, better known as the Unabomber. His hatred of modern technology and its effect on society drove him deep into the woods near Lincoln, where he built a 10-foot by 12-foot cabin and began to learn survivalist methods. He studied edible plant identification, tool and weapon construction, and how to get by with just one pair of underwear.

Kaczynski was captured, of course, when his brother David recognized the writing style and ideas presented in the Unabomber's manifesto, a 35,000-word screed published in 1995 by the *Washington*

★ ★

The trail system is located south of downtown Helena. Drive south on Park Avenue until you see the sign for Mt. Helena City Park and Reeders Village. Drive up through the subdivision on Reeders Village Drive to the dirt parking lot. It's open year round.

Post. Kaczynski's one-man "revolution against technology" came to an end after a seventeen-year bombing campaign that left three people dead and twenty-three injured. He is currently in prison doing life without parole, either working on another manifesto or writing country and western songs.

Before his capture he hunkered down in his isolated cabin for months, creating the most famous piece of work a manual typewriter has cranked out since Kerouac wrote *On the Road* in a three-week Benzedrine binge. After they nabbed him, the FBI seized the cabin and loaded it onto a flatbed, hauling it up a short logging road to a main clearing where it was whisked away by chopper. Most recently the G-men loaned out the notorious shack to Washington, D.C.'s Newseum, a 250,000-square-foot museum of the news.

Lincoln residents are still somewhat tight-lipped about the notoriety surrounding the bomb-happy hermit. The property on which the cabin sat was bought a couple of years ago and is not accessible to the public. There's not much to see anyway—the site is surrounded by a shiny, galvanized, chain-link fence that's topped by three strands of barbed wire. Nothing remains within its perimeter but overgrown bushes and vines, and the memory of one of the FBI's most elusive suspects.

If you're thinking about paying a visit, think again. Keep out. No trespassing. Stay away. The cabin might be on display, however, at the Newseum. Their Web site is www.newseum.org.

★ ★

Music to Soothe the Breast of the Savage Tourist
Nevada City

You might remember how Fonzie used to bang the malt-shop jukebox into action with a quick pop of his fist and a cool, "Heyyyy."
Well, the Fonz would probably think twice about trying that with any
of the fragile musical machinery at Nevada City's Music Hall.

The timeless building on the boardwalk of Nevada City's living
ghost town holds the world's largest collection of playable,
automatic-music machines. From player pianos to pipe organs,
the Music Hall collection is a fascinating and sometimes perplexing

Movies, Documentaries and TV Shows Filmed in Nevada City

- *Little Big Man* (1970): Dustin Hoffman plays Jack Crabb, a white
  man raised by Indians. In the movie, he looks back on an interesting life that included battling General George Armstrong
  Custer.

- *Montana Bound:* Feature film.

- *South by Northwest* (1975): Educational series about the history
  of African American settlers in the Pacific Northwest.

- *Missouri Breaks* (1976): Western starring Marlon Brando and Jack
  Nicholson.

★ ★

array of vintage machines, large and small, that were designed and built to entertain music-starved miners and pioneers.

Like Arnold's Drive-In, the Music Hall is usually bustling with people. Most pass through the Hall during their tour of the popular ghost town, which comprises dozens of faithfully restored structures. This is by far the loudest building, though, as many of the ancient instruments are still capable of putting the boom in boomtown, and stand ready to bleat and blare for the price of a few coins.

One machine even bears an old placard boasting of its status as the Loud and Obnoxious Horn Machine. "Don't miss hearing the

- *West of the Imagination* (1984–85): Six-part PBS series about the history and mythology of the American West through art and photography.

- *Gold Mountain* (1991): Feature film about a young Chinese woman sold into slavery in San Francisco. Also known as *Thousand Pieces of Gold*.

- *Unsolved Mysteries:* An episode of the popular Spike TV series was shot here.

- *Return to Lonesome Dove* (1993): TV Western miniseries starring Jon Voight and Barbara Hershey.

- *Nobody's Girls: Five Women of the West* (1994): PBS docudrama depicting the real stories of five women in the West.

- *Frontier House* (2002): Emmy-nominated miniseries depicting frontier life in 1883.

★ ★

machine that has driven 28 changemakers, 72 bartenders, and near a million tourists to the brink of insanity," it reads. The contraption contains seventeen brass horns that honk out the most eye-crossing, discordant cacophony this side of the main stage at Ozzfest.

The entire back wall of the building is taken up by a huge pipe organ that features forty-two horns, fifty pipes, and giant mechanized drums. It pounds out a Sousa march that rattles the walls.

For a fully blown mind, check out the Mills Violano-Virtuoso, a 1920s invention that actually plays the violin. Invented by Henry Sandell, this device features complex circuitry, changeable resistance, and other technological advances that were revolutionary in their time.

You can also sample several turn-of-the-century stereoscopes, viewing devices that present photos in vivid 3-D. While you're being dazzled with the images of trains and Indians, you might be serenaded with a strident tune from the Wurlitzer 180. Next to the slot where you deposit a buck to engage the immense organ, a notice reads, "Plug Your Ears." It is billed as "the loudest organ in Montana." Exactimundo.

The Music Hall is located on the Nevada City boardwalk, along MT 287. Try visiting www.virginiacitymt.com/Nevada.asp for more information.

A Heavenly Haven for Highway Hogs
Philipsburg

"Oh, I know what a serious biker needs after a 500-mile ride," growls Dave Chappell, the burly, bearded owner of the Biker Sanctuary in Philipsburg. As he leads me into his newly-repurposed Presbyterian church, visions of depravity and bad craziness dance in my head.

"He needs a hot tub, some good food, and a quality bed." He smiles sweetly, showing me the first of two comfortable, well-appointed bedrooms in P-burg's newest bed and breakfast. Indeed, the Sanctuary gives off a vibe that definitely befits the name. A sauna, two hot tubs, full cooking facilities, a game-and-exercise

★ ★

"I'm a nice guy, really. But wipe your feet if
ya know what's good for ya."

room, and a pair of snug cabins on the lawn make for a restful and
rejuvenating experience for weary bikers.

The décor inside the Sanctuary is truly remarkable, and guests are
encouraged to take their time and digest it all. Local artist Liz Silliman worked her magic throughout the building, using faux-finish
techniques to re-create patterns that Dave and his partner, Kim, had
seen in other churches, from the Vatican to the St. Ignatius Mission.

★ ★

During the three years the Chappells worked on the project, Silliman spent hundreds of hours in the renovated church, adorning the walls and floors with patterns, even painting faux bricks and trim boards to match missing sections of the originals.

Silliman also created most of the motorcycle-themed murals that adorn the walls, but these are not your Boris Vallejo–style Viking babes. One mural on a bedroom wall, *Biker's Worst Nightmare*, by Signe Johnson, depicts a pigtailed female rider coming up behind a pickup signaling a left turn.

And what if you happened to live the biker's worst nightmare and got your ride banged up? Stroll downstairs, go around back in the alley, and behind a large garage door you'll find a fully equipped machine shop, ready to cure your bike of its ills while you kick back on the deck in the eight-person hot tub, soaking your bones. And just in case two hot tubs aren't enough, Dave says they are planning to install a third one. "In the bell tower," he says, looking upward with a mischievous twinkle in his eye.

The Biker Sanctuary is on the hill overlooking downtown Philipsburg. Call (217) 248-6989 or ride past www.bikersanctuary.com.

Dig This: Crystals Up for Grabs
Polaris

Do you remember that scene in *The Sopranos* where Uncle Junior has Tony Soprano digging holes all over his backyard, trying to locate a coffee can full of mob cash he'd buried years ago? Well, that perforated yard might come to mind when you get your first gander at Crystal Park. Located along Scenic Byway 73, high in the Pioneer Mountains of the Big Hole Valley, Crystal Park is a rockhounding hot spot where, for decades, people have been digging quartz crystals out of the ground.

The resulting excavations have left the hillside looking like it's been carpet bombed. There are hundreds of pits where folks have climbed in, trowel in hand, to scrape at the soil for purple amethysts, smoky gray crystals, and other six-sided lumps of quartz. Some crystal buffs use hand-held sifters to maximize their efforts, but park rules limit diggers to hand tools only.

It's very addictive, hunkering down in your foxhole on a summer afternoon, whiling away the hours scratching through the soil, a big fat crystal always one scoopful of dirt away. Some estimates say that the supply of crystals is virtually inexhaustible, riddling the earth hundreds of feet below the surface.

How much are these glittering nuggets worth? Not much, except maybe to hippies and eccentric rock hounds. Many New Agers believe that crystals give off certain energies or cosmic vibes, and that's what gives them their value. It's all about the energy, man. No one digs at Crystal Park to turn a profit.

Amenities are minimal: two large parking lots, a couple of picnic tables, and Forest Service pit toilets. There's also a well pump where you can wet your whistle and rinse off your newly dug treasures. Best of all, there is a paved path that winds around the hillside, giving access to nearly everyone, even Uncle Junior.

To find Crystal Park, drive 3 miles south of Dillon on I-15. Take the Highway 278 exit and drive west on Highway 278 for 22 miles, then take Pioneer Mountains Scenic Byway Road 73 north for 17 miles.

Robbers Roost: It Was Full of Bad Eggs
Sheridan

Every gang worth its brass knuckles has a decent hideout—a place to lie low when the heat is on, a place to divvy up the booty from the latest heist, a place to establish the pecking order in the gang by shooting some mouthy punk in the foot.

In the Ruby Valley they had Robbers Roost, a log roadhouse built by Pete Daly in 1863. Pete wasn't a criminal himself, but he turned a blind eye to the nefarious activities of the Innocents. The ironically named Innocents was a gang led by Henry Plummer, sheriff of Bannack and Virginia City. The rest of the gang was comprised of his deputies. According to legend, Plummer and his fellow range hoods would hang out at Robbers Roost all day, waiting for travelers en route between the mining boomtowns. If they saw a party that looked like easy pickings, they would plan an ambush in one of the many unprotected, wilderness spots between the mining camps.

In another huge wad of irony, Plummer and his bloodthirsty boys were captured and hanged by the Vigilantes in 1864.

The log building you can visit today is not the original Robbers Roost; this one was constructed several years after Plummer and his men were forced to dance at the end of a rope. This newer building, built on the same site as the original, initially had a much more legitimate function: serving as a traditional stage stop.

As for Pete Daly, he lived to a ripe old age and was one of the valley's most prominent citizens at the time of his death in 1915. Even though he unwittingly provided the road agents with a hideout, Daly was never directly involved with their criminal endeavors and was spared any repercussions from the law. Hmm. Maybe he should have run for Congress.

Robbers Roost is located about 5 miles southeast of Sheridan on MT 287.

For Fun, Find the Floating Flotilla and Fish Fantasies
Twin Bridges

In late July the waters of the Beaverhead River are flowing slow and clear through the town of Twin Bridges. It's the beginning of the hay harvest, and folks are looking forward to a day of craziness and whimsy to help blow off a growing-season's worth of steam.

Hence the Floating Flotilla and Fish Fantasies river parade.

People come from all over the area to line the banks of the river next to the fairgrounds. They perch in their folding chairs, coolers and cameras close at hand. Before long the flotilla begins to make its way around the bend in the river and into full view of the crowd. The lead craft is a canoe bearing a man waving a huge U.S. flag in the

★ ★

bow while, in the stern, a guy blows on a wooden train whistle. The flotilla is officially under way.

People might work all spring building their wacky watercraft, or some may throw something together a couple of hours before the event. All kinds of non-motorized crafts are represented, from inner tubes to fly-fishing pontoons and rowboats. Contestants decorate

This is the only time of year you'll see a Viking ship on the Beaverhead River.

★ ★

them up to look like all kinds of things. Tropical islands have been spotted. Viking ships have been known to make an appearance, and there was even a blue whale complete with spouting blowhole. It's all entertaining, and watching the contestants and their crazy boats trying to navigate their way down the waist-deep river has the crowd laughing nonstop. Flotilla riders (flotillants?) dress in crazy costumes or wear big goofy hats, adding to the wild and wooly proceedings.

The flotilla proceeds under the bridge near the foot of the water tower and takes out just past there in a city park. A few floaters run into trouble, however, when they disregard the organizers' warnings about the bridge height and water-level measurements. Scofflaw sailors have been known to wreck their boats when a tall mast or errant decoration smashes into the bridge, usually sending the occupants into the drink while the spectators applaud wildly.

Who said farmers don't know how to have fun?

For more information, call (406) 842-7688 or go to www.sheridan wired.com.

Yo, Adrian! You Seen My Nuts?
Virginia City

There are two historical museums in the "living ghost town" of Virginia City, and they're both free (donations accepted). The Virginia City Historical Museum in the middle of town is worth a look mostly for its taxidermy. The fine collection includes a two-headed calf, a lamb-and-a-half, and the crown jewel of the collection, a pair of boxing squirrels.

The calf and lamb are on display in the upstairs, gift-shop portion of the establishment. The double-skulled calf is one of quite a few specimens scattered across the state. The lamb is kind of creepy: six legs, four ears, and two bodies. It stands in a display case on the front counter of the store. You have to go downstairs to enter the museum, which is chock full of the typical, pioneer-museum stuff. You got your old photos, your buckboard wagon, saddles and tack,

RED & GRAY SQUIRREL

I'm guessing the taxidermist was a fan of the sweet science. Or *Over the Hedge.*

★ ★

various iron farming implements, vintage organs, and other detritus from days gone by. There's a nifty display depicting the office of *The Madisonian*, Montana's oldest continuously operated weekly paper, established in 1873.

But the wildlife taxidermy collection, donated by Mrs. Irene Martin, is the most entertaining section of the museum. Some of the

Nicknames Were Cruel in the Old West

"Clubfoot" George Lane was a boot maker in Virginia City. As you might guess, he had a deformed foot. Lane, originally from Massachusetts, had come west in search of gold in the 1860s. He worked his way through California, Washington, and Idaho before finally setting foot in Virginia City in 1863.

Dogged by accusations of horse thievery, Lane set up shop in Dance and Stuwart's Store, mending harnesses and making and repairing boots. You could say he was trying to put his best foot forward. And while he made a comfortable living, it would be a stretch to say he was well-heeled.

During this time, Henry Plummer's gang, the Innocents, were operating out of Bannack. A vigilante movement was gathering in Virginia City, and Plummer was in their sights. For some reason, Lane took it upon himself to ride to Bannack to warn Plummer to keep on his toes. His affiliation with the gang was soon discovered, and Clubfoot George was arrested for being a spy and a road agent. "If you

★ ★

taxidermy is pretty good, although some is honestly kind of clumsy (two flattened ducks look like freshly harvested roadkill, and a bald eagle has a steel rod sticking out of its head).

In addition to the tiny boxing ring containing the shorts-clad, boxing-gloved squirrels, there are all kinds of other wildlife mounts. There's a deer, an antelope, a badger, a fox, and a . . . cow?

hang me," he reportedly said, "you will hang an innocent man." The trial was swift; Clubfoot didn't have a leg to stand on.

He was strung up alongside four other convicted criminals, and all five were buried unceremoniously in Virginia City's Boot Hill cemetery. There were no grave markers. Clubfoot maintained his innocence right up to the end, trying to convince anyone who would listen that he'd always toed the line.

Some forty-three years after the burials, questions began to arise as to the identities of the men buried with no markers. A former Vigilante claimed to remember who was in which grave, and to prove it he had the city dig up Clubfoot George's grave. Sure enough, there was his deformed foot, now just bones.

The bones are on display under a glass dome at the Thompson Hickman Museum in Virginia City. And if that's not creepy enough for you, ask to see the one-hundred-year-old cake or the mummified cat. You'll get a kick out of them.

The Thompson Hickman Museum is located at 215 East Idaho Street in Virginia City. To learn more, tiptoe to the phone and call (406) 843-5238.

Granted, the head of a cow seems a little out of place, but when a collection contains a pair of rodent Rocky Balboas, you tend to keep your questions to yourself.

The Virginia City Historical Museum is located at 219 Wallace Street. Their phone number is (406) 843-5500.

The Best Place for Hard Rock Music
Whitehall

If you round a corner on a winding gravel road south of Butte and come upon some people tapping on large rocks with hammers, do not be alarmed. These are not crack-brained prospectors, they're just enjoying the bell-like tones of the Ringing Rocks.

This large pile of reddish gray boulders, some as big as riding lawnmowers, is an ultra-rare geological formation that can be found in only two other places on Earth. The rocks chime when tapped lightly with a hammer. Each rock has a different tone, sometimes a "ting," sometimes a "tong," and there's an occasional "tang." One theory is that the ringing is a combination of the composition of the rock and the way the joining patterns have developed as the rocks have eroded away.

Visitors will find worn areas on many of the rocks where they have been hammered on over the years. If a boulder is removed from the pile, however, it doesn't ring. (This may or may not be some sort of natural defense mechanism, I'm not sure.)

In 1965 a geologist removed a few rocks from one of the other sites, in Pennsylvania (the third is in Australia), and took them to his lab to find out what makes them ring. Although the rocks don't ring when removed from the pile, he did discover that tones were still produced, albeit in frequencies too low to be heard by the human ear. He concluded that the tones interacting with each other produced overtones that were audible.

★ ★

A couple of helpful notes: The gravel road, although nicely maintained, gets increasingly treacherous as you near the site. The last 200 yards are peppered with large, jagged rocks waiting to gouge a hole in your oil pan. A high-clearance vehicle is recommended, but there is a spot for parking if you want to walk the last bit.

Also, don't forget to bring a hammer. I had forgotten mine during my first visit, and the only object in the car I could find to strike the rocks with was an aluminum baseball bat. It's the absolute worst implement I could have used, because everything I hit with it, of course, made a "ting." Rocks, trees, my car's windshield, everything.

To play a few notes of your own rock and roll, take exit 241 off I-90 near Pipestone. Go under the overpasses and head east on the gravel road for about 0.8 mile, then turn north on the gravel road (there should be a sign). Cross the railroad tracks, and go for another 3.5 miles. There is an informational sign at the Ringing Rocks.

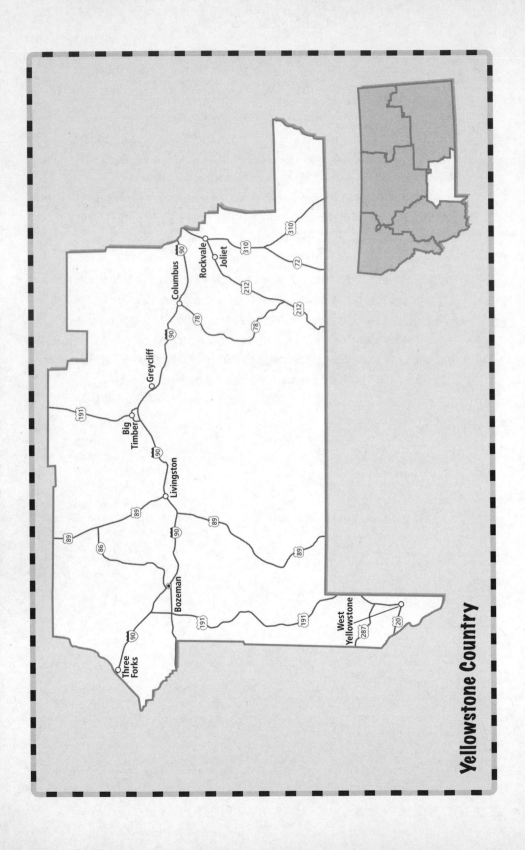

Yellowstone Country

Yellowstone Country

A lot of *people call it God's country, this area just north of Yellowstone Park. If you can make it up the Paradise Valley without being recruited by the ambitiously named Church Universal and Triumphant, you'll find yourself in Livingston, the town that Jimmy Buffet sings about in "Livingston Saturday Night." Just up the road lives another famous celebrity, Brutus the grizzly bear. He's at the Grizzly Bear Encounter roadside exhibit just outside of Bozeman.*

Bozeman, once a sleepy cowboy town, is now a bustling hub of college, commerce, and skiing. Gary Cooper went to high school there, and it's also the home of Big Red, the last ox to pull freight across the Bozeman Trail. Well, it's home to his head, anyway. While in the Bozone, as the locals call it, you can also see wildlife of the stainless steel variety, created by local artist Jim Dolan.

Hollywood loves Yellowstone Country, and it's not just for its thespian bears. Big Timber will look familiar if you've seen The Horse Whisperer *or* A River Runs Through It. *A number of actors also live in the area, and you might even catch Kevin Costner or Dennis Quaid leading their respective rock bands at some local watering hole. Tip: do not request "Freebird."*

The scenery is among the most beautiful in the state, to be sure. But from Belfry (local ball team: the Bats) to Big Sky (the brainchild of newsman Chet Huntley), Yellowstone Country also has its share of stuff that will make you go, "Huh?"

★ ★

A Movie Runs Through It
Big Timber

Big Timber, just east of Livingston, epitomizes the collective consciousness of what Montana should look like. It looks so much like the essence of the Treasure State that two major Hollywood movies were filmed in and around the picturesque western town.

Hometown of Montana's first female governor, Judy Martz, Big Timber is an ideal sheep ranching area, and at one time produced more wool than anywhere else in the nation. Sheep ranching has since been replaced by farming, however, and occasional moviemaking. Nearby Livingston is a popular Montana haven for the Hollywood set, and Big Timber residents are used to occasionally rubbing shoulders with the odd movie star. I suppose that would include sportscaster Brent Musburger, who was raised there.

A River Runs Through It (1992) and *The Horse Whisperer* (1998) both did pretty well at the box office, giving millions of moviegoers their first glimpse of Big Sky Country. Even though *A River Runs Through It* was supposedly set in Missoula, Big Timber served as a stand-in for the mountain-ringed college town. Even the Blackfoot River, which is quite beautiful in its own right, was replaced by the Boulder and Yellowstone Rivers, near Big Timber.

Robert Redford directed both films, and he approached the second movie with some lessons learned after completing the first. He provided the cast and crew with manuals on how to deal with Montanans (I'm guessing number one: Deny you're from California), and injected a large production budget into the local economy. Jack Fuller, owner of the Timber Bar, was one of the many Big Timber residents who benefitted directly from the movie shoot. "We had the worst year in thirty-nine years," he said shortly after shooting was finished. "But this (movie) is pulling us out."

Big Timber was not mentioned in the credits of *Whisperer*, which reportedly cheesed off a few locals. But Redford made the decision to keep the town's identity on the down-low after *A River Runs Through It* brought a deluge of fly-fishing wannabes flooding into the quiet towns and streams of western Montana.

If you're planning on passing through the Big Timber area, it might be a good idea to rent the pair of Redford modern western epics, and see if you can recognize the many location sets in one of the most beautiful corners of Montana.

Big Timber lies along I-90, 60 miles east of Bozeman.

At Least the Greeks Didn't Have to Deal with windows Vista
Bozeman

When Steve Jobs and Steve Wozniak were building the first Apple computer in Jobs's garage in 1976, they probably didn't stop to think that the road leading to their invention began some 20,000 years ago.

A trip to Bozeman's American Computer Museum would have provided those digital pioneers with some perspective. A surprisingly complete collection tucked into a strip mall at the north end of Seventh Avenue, the museum might more accurately be called the Museum of Human Communication.

The tour starts with a twelve-minute film that sets the tone for the displays, which are arranged in chronological order. Then, after a quick intro to the concept of binary code, you're off into the museum. The first displays feature prehistoric cave paintings and replicas of 4,000-year-old Babylonian tablets, along with explanations of how these were used to communicate ideas and information among early human cultures.

Perhaps the museum's most stunning display, however, is a reconstruction of the Antikythera mechanism, a 2,000-year-old Greek device that's been acknowledged as the world's earliest existing computer.

The displays progress through a detailed replica of the Gutenberg press, antique books on language and science, and a collection of early number crunchers like the abacus. There's even an early

★ ★

calculator called Tate's Arithmometer: a complex but elegant, 2-foot-long, wood-and-brass box arrayed with rows of levers and buttons. Imagine having to tote that thing to calculus class.

You'll learn about Herman Hollerith, the father of modern data processing. He started a little company called IBM. From there you'll take a tour of the modern computer age, from a room-size Univac to a large collection of pocket calculators.

It's not all business, either. The museum has an amazing example of the very first arcade video game and a collection of home video

This amount of computing power is now contained in your average musical greeting card.

systems. Be prepared for a 1970s flashback when you see Atari's Pong.

There's even a diorama featuring a painted backdrop of a head-band-wearing hippie sitting under a Led Zeppelin poster, presumably working on that first Apple; it featured a wood case and the groovy name "Apple Is." Far out, man.

The American Computer Museum is located at 2304 North Seventh Avenue. Call (406) 582-1288 or type www.compustory.com into your Web browser.

You'll Need More Than a Stairmaster to Prepare for This Run
Bozeman

The "runner's high." That's the physiological phenomenon enjoyed by joggers and road racers when they reach a certain point of exertion where their body starts pumping endorphins, giving them a feeling of euphoria. But don't hold your breath waiting for it to hit if you're running in Bozeman's notorious Ridge Run. If your mind wanders for even a moment, you might fall off a mountain.

The Ed Anacker Bridger Ridge Run, as it's known, is a grueling test of physical fortitude that makes the Ironman Triathlon look like a tiptoe through the tulips. Anacker, a Montana State University professor, began the event in 1985 as a torturous challenge to the most intrepid outdoor athletes. A field of 300 runners tackles the 20-mile course each August, and it is one of the most punishing events of its kind in the world.

Runners have to keep their focus on the terrain directly in front of them, or risk certain disaster. There is no actual trail to follow as they climb nearly a mile straight up a mountainside, scrambling over shin-gouging scree, and then run the length of Bridger Ridge (including 9,600-foot Sacajawea Peak) before they descend to the parking lot below the big "M."

Blisters, cuts, scrapes, sprained ankles, and the occasional broken bone are all part of the Ridge Run, which is hosted by the Wind

Drinkers, a Bozeman running organization. The unpredictable south-west Montana weather is also a factor, bringing anything from a sun-burn to a freak snowstorm. Give it a try if you feel up to it, but you know, Lewis and Clark went around this thing for a reason.

Lace up those Nikes and trot over to www.winddrinkers.org for more information.

Heavy Metal on the Hoof
Bozeman

As you enter Bozeman from the west, you might be startled by a large herd of elk feeding on a landscaped knoll at First Interstate Bank. They're always there. They never leave. They can't. They're made of steel mesh.

Belgrade-based artist Jim Dolan, a renowned wildlife sculptor, cre-ated the larger-than-life herd in 1985, and they have been causing double-takes ever since. The tableau is that of a proud bull protect-ing his harem from a large interloper. The bull's antlers are tipped in gleaming stainless steel, which makes them look mighty fearsome indeed.

Upon closer inspection, you can see that the rump sections of the elk are also stainless steel, so while the rest of the sculpture has turned reddish brown with oxidation over the years, the rump stayed silver, giving the elk an even more lifelike appearance. Dolan is cel-ebrated for such attention to detail in his metal sculptures of eagles, horses, bison, and other Montana wildlife.

You can experience another of Dolan's stunning wildlife installa-tions a mere 10 miles from the Bozeman elk. In the main terminal of Gallatin Field Airport, an airborne flock of geese floats frozen high overhead. The geese seem to be flying away from the baggage claim area, which means they are either traveling light or the airline has lost their luggage.

The ten life-size birds, which dominate the airspace of the central terminal, are arranged as if they're coming in for a landing, suspended by cables directly above the stone staircase. The detail, proportional accuracy, and uncanny body positioning look like the real thing. Let's just hope they don't poop rivets.

Bozeman's First Interstate Bank is located at 2800 West Main Street.

"These buns of steel can be a real pain in the winter!"

You've Got to Be Cool as a Cucumber to Tackle This Ice

You say mere rock climbing has become too mundane, too simple, not nearly the life-threatening adventure you need to elevate your pulse and tighten your pucker string? Well, you and your thrill-seeking brethren (and sisteren) have an exciting opportunity awaiting in Bozeman.

Welcome to the chilly winter sport of ice climbing. The Bozeman Ice Festival takes place in December of each year, and focuses attention on this lunatic, I mean, adventurous combination of rock climbing and trying not to freeze to death.

The festival has been going on for fifteen years, and organizers encourage climbers of all ages and abilities to come out and learn about climbing techniques, new developments in equipment and clothing, and all kinds of helpful information about this dangerous but exhilarating sport.

The Icebreaker Pro Invitational Competition, held on the spectacular frozen waterfalls and chutes of Hyalite Canyon, just south of Bozeman, attracts some of the world's greatest ice climbers.

Even if the closest you ever come to ice climbing is drinking your whiskey on the rocks, you'll get a thrill out of watching these maniacs, that is, athletes conquer one of the most exciting (did I mention dangerous?) winter challenges in Montana.

For more information about ice locations, lodging, and other frosty details, rappel your way down to www.montanaice.com.

* *

Hot Food, a Soft Bed, and the Ghost of Gary Cooper
Bozeman

Hollywood-minded travelers caught between the national parks of Yellowstone and Glacier might want to bivouac in Bozeman. There's a chance they could hang their hats in the home where Oscar-winning actor Gary Cooper grew up.

The Bozeman Backpackers Hostel is the current iteration of the charming, 120-year-old Victorian house on Olive Street. Before Cooper gained fame as the stoic sheriff in *High Noon* (and other movies), he attended Gallatin High School in Bozeman and lived in this quiet, tree-lined neighborhood just a few blocks from downtown.

The hostel was opened in 1991, and has hosted thousands of footloose travelers from all over the world. Owner Wayne Mortimer credits the hostel's popularity to its relaxed attitude. The doors are not locked during the day, there is no curfew, and all they ask is a respectful attitude toward the hostel and its guests.

People take turns preparing potluck meals in the kitchen. The nights frequently bring lively game-playing or music jam sessions, depending on the mix of visitors. The spacious front porch provides a relaxing atmosphere to kick back and take in the Bozeman vibe.

Mortimer came home to the hostel one night to find that twenty-three Colombians had moved into the house. It turned out they were Yellowstone National Park workers stopping for the night on their way to the park. The hostel officially sleeps only fifteen people, but they threw some mattresses on the floor and everyone got some shuteye.

If you stay at the hostel, you might be lucky enough to actually bunk in Gary Cooper's original bedroom. His picture and some news articles adorn the walls, so there's no doubt which room it is. And when you hear that train whistle blow, relax. It's probably just the Burlington Northern, not gunman Frank Miller coming to take his revenge.

The Bozeman Backpackers Hostel is on 405 West Olive Street. You can call (406) 586-4659 for more information or visit their Web site, www.bozemanbackpackershostel.com.

Please, Keep Your Chewing Gum Jokes to Yourself
Bozeman

Inside Powder Horn Sportsman's Supply, Bozeman's finest sporting goods emporium, you'll find dozens of big game mounts on the walls. The sheer variety of animals is amazing, with everything from a sailfish to a musk ox staring down at you from their eternal reward.

Is anyone else feeling , um, you know. What's that word? Starts with an H . . .

★ ★

But the most famous head by far is Big Red the Ox. In true, no-nonsense pioneer fashion, Big Red got his name because he was big. And red. The last ox to pull a load of freight over the famed Bozeman Trail, he's probably the most renowned ox since Mongo's mount in *Blazing Saddles*.

The Bozeman Trail was an integral part of the settlement of southwestern Montana. Eventually it became part of a transcontinental railroad route that was used by the Northern Pacific Railroad to connect Minnesota to the Pacific Northwest.

After his death in 1910, Big Red was stuffed and mounted by some historically minded Bozeman residents. They later donated the business end to George Dieruf, original owner of the Powder Horn. To this day Big Red looks out from his place on the wall near the back of the store, his thousand-yard stare betraying nothing. A small sign identifies the ox and his place in history, and Powder Horn employees are happy to fill you in on his legend. And yes, they are aware of the chewing gum of the same name.

Bozeman's Powder Horn Sportsman's Supply and Big Red are both on 35 East Main Street. Call (406) 587-7373 to find out more.

You Want Fish? We Got Your Trout Where They Can't Get Out
Bozeman

If you're an angler or even if you just like to watch fish, there's a great opportunity for you to see a few hundred mature rainbow trout up close and personal, just outside of Bozeman.

The Fish Technology Center is located at the entrance to Bridger Canyon on Davies Spring Creek. It began as one of the first fish hatcheries in the National Fish Hatchery System in 1897. The hatchery initially produced steelhead and brook trout, and soon began stocking local waters. There's even record of Buffalo Bill Cody requesting trout and grayling for some waters on his Wyoming ranch.

★ ★

Today, though, the hatchery has evolved into a Fish Cultural Development Center. They deal with such issues as water-treatment systems, hatchery affluent, sedimentation facilities, carrying capacity and rearing methods, diet testing, brood stock research, and many other scientific-sounding subjects.

The center no longer produces fish for stocking local fisheries, but you can tour the facility and see what kind of research they're doing. It's an interesting tour, to be sure, but if you want to commune directly with the main attractions, just step outside. There's a holding pond in the campus-like facility, and it's boiling with large, healthy rainbow trout. These aren't your typical hatchery denizens, either. No stunted fins, concrete fungi, flattened noses, or bad attitudes. These beautiful specimens are vital and feisty. If you walk around the pond, they'll follow you like cattle in a pen, waiting for you to toss some food. A posted sign forbids throwing anything into the pond, though, so feeding the fish is definitely verboten.

For a fisherman, however, it's hard to resist the temptation to throw a little something in the pond; something like, say, a Panther Martin spinner or a dry fly.

The Bozeman Fish Technology Center is located at the entrance to Bridger Canyon, about 4 miles northeast of Bozeman on MT 86. They're open from 8:30 a.m. to 4 p.m., Monday through Friday. To catch a big experience, call (406) 587-9265 or visit www.fws.gov/bozemanfishtech.

Griz Fans, Here's the Real Thing
Bozeman

There are a handful of Hollywood types that famously make their homes in the Big Sky state, and southwest Montana seems to have more than its fair share, from Dennis Quaid to Peter Fonda. One such actor, who had a key role in the 2009 movie *Did You Hear About the Morgans?*, makes his home near Bozeman. He weighs around 900 pounds and spends most of his time sleeping and eating.

No, they're not fighting, they're playing.
You know how siblings are.

★ ★

Trivia

Montana is hung up on Big. It is, of course, the Big Sky state, but there's also Big Hole, Big Ice Cave, Big Mountain, Big Arm, Big Open, Big Sag, Big Belt Mountains, Big Timber, Bigfork and Big Horn. Oddly, Mississippi bluesman Big Bill Broonzy has never set foot in Montana. Weird.

No, it's not Marlon Brando; it's Brutus the grizzly bear. He's the star attraction at Montana Grizzly Encounter, a tourist-friendly sanctuary for rescued grizzlies. Brutie, as the Encounter trainers call him, is eight years old, and a well-trained veteran of TV and movies. He's appeared on *Oprah*, as well as a *National Geographic* series on majestic bears of the American West.

Along with four other bears currently at the facility, Brutus plays an important part in educating the public about grizzlies. Ami Testa and bear-trainer Casey Anderson opened the Grizzly Encounter to provide a place to rehabilitate and train grizzlies rescued from bad captivity situations. "These bears are beyond spoiled," says Ami. "There's no way they could ever be released into the wild."

The bears spend their days frolicking in the expansive, forested habitat. It's complete with rolling knolls of grass, a few pine trees, a 7-foot-deep swimming hole, and two waterfalls. Visitors can view the bears from just across a safety barrier. Mom and Dad can sit or stand on huge log benches while they take photos and videos of the playful critters.

Each bear has his or her own den, and they tend to keep to their own schedules, not forced to perform or do tricks. It's not a zoo and it's not really a wildlife park. It's almost like a little piece of bear paradise where the grizzlies enjoy plenty of treats and pampering.

Brutus and his buddies each eat up to thirty-five pounds of food a day, and it costs around $10,000 per month to run the facility. The Encounter has attained nonprofit status, and accepts donations from the public. There is also a small fee to enter the park, but you can stay as long as you like. Brutus will let you know when it's time to go.

East of Bozeman, the Grizzly Encounter is accessible from I-90 at 80 Bozeman Hill Road. If you want to get down to the bear essentials, call (406) 586-8893 or lumber over to www.grizzlyencounter.com.

That Coat Must Really Show the Dirt

Columbus

Mule deer and whitetailed deer are abundant in Montana, but you probably will never get the chance to see a rare albino deer. That is, unless you stop in to the New Atlas Bar in Columbus.

The bar itself is an eye-popping experience given its dozens of wild game mounts lining the walls. Everything from a rattlesnake to a moose is represented here, some with head mounts others with just the skull on a shelf. Ancient ceiling fans whirl beneath the stamped-tin ceiling, and there are not one but two huge, ornate old back bars. One of them has "Welcome Stranger" painted on the center mirror next to a portrait of a cowboy riding a bucking bronc.

But the snow white deer is given the place of honor, mounted in a glass display case smack dab in the middle of the bar, just above the vintage upright piano. With its huge ears and its caught-in-the-head-lights look on its face, the animal appears to be normal in all respects but its color. If it weren't for the pink eyes, you might just wonder if this critter had stumbled into a vat of peroxide or maybe tangled with a highway paint truck.

The New Atlas Bar is located at 528 East Pike Avenue in Columbus.

Direct Your Snow Prayers to the Ski God Creature

When Chuck Ringer was a five-year-old lad living in Minnesota, he would pull his red wagon a mile and a half to the town dump, filling the wagon with a pile of interesting junk before taking it home to build stuff.

Some fifty years later Chuck is making a comfortable living doing the same thing. Only instead of junk from the dump, he works mostly with steel, iron, and aluminum, creating a series of fantastical, whimsical, sometimes-puzzling but always-stunning works of art in his Joliet studio.

"People think there are two artists here," he says with a twinkle in his eye. One artist is the man who creates the smooth, polished, high-end art that sells for as much as five figures. These pieces can sometimes contain hundreds of welds and take several months to complete. They populate his airy gallery and draw oohs and ahhs from the travelers brave enough to stop for the "Art Crossing" sign and come inside for a look.

The other artist is the adult version of that five-year-old dump digger who scavenges all kinds of metal and other castoffs to assemble some hilariously twisted art. His *Steel Toed Boots*, for example, is a battered pair of cowboy boots, each with a stainless steel big toe poking up through the leather. One of his more recent creations is a full-size flying saucer, complete with a crew of aliens who have debarked in order to examine their surroundings.

It's this "second artist" who created Ringer's most popular piece, the *Ski God Creature*. Also called the Ooga Booga Man, the 18-foot-tall steel doofus Ringer built in 1982 stands in the yard next to the highway. He's known as Ula by the snowboarders who have adopted him as their patron saint of awesome powder. They stop on their way to the local ski area, and toss money at the statue as an offering. Ringer has picked up over $500 from the lawn in the last few years. He plans on using the money to fund a speaker/microphone system in the creature so the artist can watch the supplicants from behind a mirrored window in his studio and provide a voice to the statue.

"I'll say, 'If you want snow, don't throw change. Throw ten-dollar bills!'" he laughs.

The Charles Ringer Studio and Gallery is located at 418 East Front Street in Joliet. Call (406) 962-3705 to talk about making a tribute to the snow gods, or schuss by www.charlesringer.com.

"Greetings, mortals. I am now accepting sacrifices of imported beer, traveler's checks, Krugerrands . . ."

★ ★

Not a Good Place for Whack-A-Mole
Greycliff

Anyone who's ever seen *Caddyshack* will tell you that gophers are cute. They might not all be fabulous dancers like Bill Murray's nemesis in the golf movie, but they can be very entertaining.

Which brings us to the Las Vegas of rodent cities, Greycliff Prairie Dog Town near Big Timber. The ninety-eight-acre state park is home to thousands of black-footed prairie dogs, a curious and highly animated critter.

When you watch dozens of foot-long rodents constantly popping up on their hind legs to chirp and peek out from their burrows, you'll see why the term "prairie-dogging" has entered the lexicon of cubical-office culture. They're kind of shy, though, and they'll disappear underground if you get closer than 10 or 12 feet. Make sure you bring a zoom lens and some binoculars.

For an untended dog of the canine variety, this place represents Disneyland, a free buffet, and Christmas morning all rolled into one. Don't forget: All dogs must be kept on a leash at all times.

The park is for daytime use only, and the parking area is wheelchair accessible. The prairie dogs are active year-round, but summer makes for the best viewing.

Greycliff Prairie Dog Town State Monument is located 9 miles east of Big Timber on I-90. Take the Greycliff exit and, as you pull into the parking lot, try to remember your favorite lines from *Caddyshack*.

Armed Giant Beckons Gamblers
Rockvale

Oh, that Muffler Man. His brawny clones are scattered around the country, all in an identical pose. The only thing that differentiates them is their dress and what they're holding in their giant hands.

The 20-foot-tall cowboy in Rockvale stands like a sentry near the intersection of US 310 and US 212, cradling a rifle as his steely gaze lets you know that he means business.

Hey, he puts on his pants one leg at a time like you.
It just takes a lot longer.

★ ★

This particular Muffler Man is designed to draw customers into the casino behind him. The joint is made up to look like a nineteenth-century frontier fort, complete with blazing cannons poking out between the turrets on the roof. It all seems vaguely menacing, as though the metal giant is suggesting that you get in there and drop some coin if you know what's good for you.

The Casino Muffler Man stands guard at the junction of US 310 and US 212 in Rockvale. Smile when you say, "Change for a five."

Let's Get Out of Here Before Batman Comes Home
Three Forks

Deep underground in a limestone hill near Three Forks, the Lewis and Clark Caverns lure thousands of visitors each year to one of the state's most popular attractions. The famed explorers themselves, though, never actually set foot in the caves. The caverns weren't even discovered until 1892, nearly a century after the Corps of Discovery had left for the East.

But no matter. You'll feel more like Indiana Jones than Meriwether Lewis when you descend some 400 feet into the cool, dark expanse of caverns. The tour begins with a steep, half-mile-long hike up an asphalt trail to the cave entrance where state park rangers give guided tours from May to September. Most of the rangers are quite garrulous and well-informed. Perhaps more entertaining than the official tour spiel is the variety of questions asked by confused tourists:

"How much of the cave is actually underground?"

"Are those vampire bats? How do they know when the sun comes up?"

"Why do they keep it so cold in here?"

"Why didn't they build it closer to the Interstate?"

My personal favorite came from a teenage girl after the tour ranger pointed out a textured wall they refer to as "cave popcorn."

"Is that where they got the idea for those ceilings in my grand-mother's house?" she asked.

The final chamber of the tour is called the Great Hall, and it is loaded with spectacular formations, all of which have some kind of obvious name. (This one is called the "Louisville Slugger." That one is the "Empire State Building." Over there is the "Rock-Shaped Rock.") They have installed white LED lighting that allows the full spectrum of color to be revealed in the formations. It's a great payoff after an hour of monochromatic geology.

Lewis and Clark Caverns State Park is 22 miles west of Three Forks on MT 2, or 18 miles east of Whitehall on MT 2. Delve into http://fwp.mt.gov/lands/site_281895.aspx for more information.

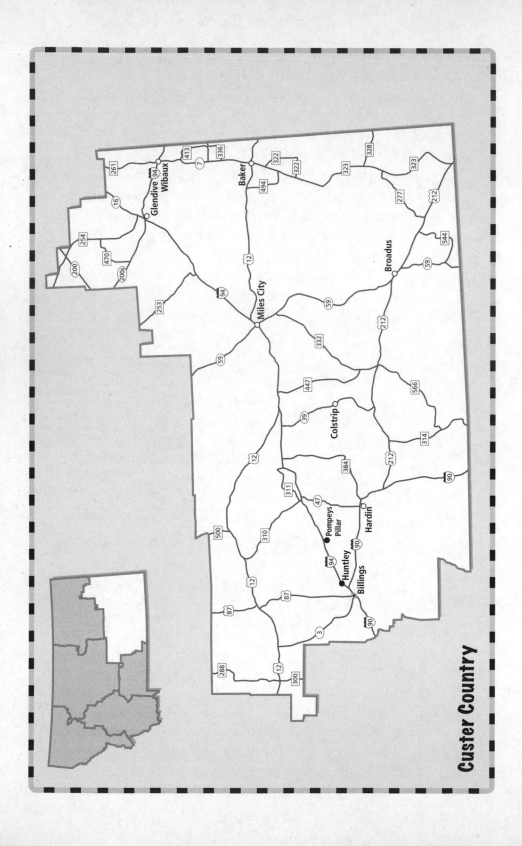

Custer Country

4

Custer Country

Each year in June there's an event that leaves no doubt that you're in Custer Country. It's the reenactment of the Battle of Little Big Horn, formerly known as Custer's Last Stand. As history now shows, it wasn't much of a stand at all—more of an extremely personal history lesson for Gen. George Armstrong Custer.

Billings, Montana's biggest city, is a good jumping-off point. If you're downtown, check out the kinetic sculpture, Skypoint, and keep your eyes peeled for the bizarre, iron sculptures by local artist Lyndon Fayne Pomeroy. Like much of eastern Montana, this area's also prime dinosaur country. You can see the fossilized skeleton of a duck-billed dinosaur in Ekalaka and, in Glendive, they have their very own statue of the Glendisaurus, loosely based on the popular triceratops. Very loosely.

For sheer curiosity potential you can't go wrong with the Range Riders Museum in Miles City. It's a sprawling collection of vintage cowboy stuff, quirky pioneer remnants, and some highly detailed dioramas. And bagpipes.

Custer Country, with the Crow and Cheyenne Indian reservations hard against Montana's southern border, truly is a land of wide-open spaces and history dating back millions of years. In Broadus, 1,100 miles from the ocean, you can view a colossal collection of seashells. And that's only the tip of the conch. You never know what lies around the next corner in the southeast corner of the state.

He's the World's Largest Steer, and That's No Bull

Baker

A rancher with no apparent imagination saddled him with the name Steer Montana. It was a simple, short name for what may have been the biggest steer ever. This bovine behemoth weighed as much as 4,280 pounds at his peak, and was 3,890 pounds when he died in 1938 at the well-cured age of sixteen. He was stuffed, mounted, and put on display in all his beefy glory at the O'Fallon Historical Museum in Baker.

To put it in perspective, a typical steer is fully grown at about eighteen months, and might tip the scales at 1,800 pounds. S. M. truly was the King Kong of steers. At 10 feet, 4 inches long, he was just a nose shorter than a Mini Cooper. He stood 5 feet, 11 inches at the shoulder, and had a girth of 9 feet and 4 inches. If a steer this size were butchered, a porterhouse steak would be the size of a trash can lid.

His owner, Jack Guth, pretty much made a career out of traveling the county with S. M., showing him at county fairs, circuses, and rodeos. S. M. was reportedly quite docile, allowing kids to climb on him and even walk underneath him. He never batted a baseball-size eye. He had two brothers, Bulgy and Spot, who were also pretty sizeable. No one knows exactly what made these particular animals grow so large, but one clue might be in their feed. It seems Jack had a still and made excellent whiskey, and fed the mash to the steers. The animals had the same mother but were sired by different bulls, so the mash is the only common element to their upbringing.

The expertly mounted steer was donated to the museum in memory of Bernie Heiser after being displayed for a while in his Heiser Bar. If you make it to the museum to see S. M., ask if you can go next door and see something even more amazing: his reconstructed skeleton. Moo!

The O'Fallon Historical Museum is at 723 South Main Street in Baker. Call (406) 778-3265 to ask them, "Where's the beef?"

It Points! At the Sky! Get It?
Billings

Smack dab in the middle of downtown Billings, *Skypoint* towers some
73 feet over the intersection of Second Avenue and Broadway. The
144-ton kinetic sculpture dominates the busy intersection, looking
somewhat like a troop of skydivers got tangled up in a rollercoaster.

A curving, white-pipe framework stretches up the sides of the
corner buildings, and three "sails" make up the roof of the structure.
The largest sail can move to let the sun through or to cover the intersection if it rains. *Skypoint* was conceived as part of a larger plan to
revitalize downtown Billings and attract more people to the area.

The structure, originally saddled with the stodgy name, *Defining
Element*, was completed in April 2002 and dedicated a month later.

I don't know, it seems like an odd place to pitch a tent.

★ ★

Trivia

In 1993 the town of Ismay (population twenty-six) renamed itself Joe to honor the NFL quarterback. That's right, Joe Montana. He's reportedly never visited there, much to Ismay's dismay.

It was built as a new icon for the city of Billings and has been used to provide shade for events such as the Strawberry Festival, the Christmas Stroll, and other happenings.

Skypoint was given its name by seventh-grader Elizabeth Burley, who submitted the moniker in a contest sponsored by the Downtown Billings Association. Some of the losing entries included *The Inside Of My Couch*, *Aretha Franklin's Hat*, and *Cat's Cradle On Acid*.

Since its unveiling, *Skypoint* has been a lightning rod for both criticism and praise. Some residents call it an eyesore (and worse), while others hail it as a much-needed shot of personality for Montana's largest city. You'll just have to judge for yourself.

Skypoint is located at the intersection of Second Avenue and Broadway, in downtown Billings.

The Men of Steel
Billings

They stand sure-footed and broad-shouldered, gazing toward the eastern sunrise. Perhaps they are dreaming of the communist ideals that once flourished in Stalinist Russia. Or maybe they're just hoping to pull a tranny.

Statues for the Proletariat is a highfalutin name for the *Transmission Titan* and *Front End Man*, two iron giants that stand between the street and a pair of auto repair businesses in Billings. The alignment

"Mom, it followed me home. Can I keep it?"

★ ★

shop's statue holds the front-end assembly from some long-forgotten car, chrome rims dangling on an axle like a Detroit barbell. The Tranny Titan, with his sheet-metal work apron, cradles a transmission like it's a newborn babe.

The squared-off, idealized style of the statues is highly reminiscent of Soviet-era propaganda posters and sculptures, suggesting a willingness to endure back-breaking labor in order to serve the greater good. Billings artist Lyndon Fayne Pomeroy created the pair of working stiffs, but it's not clear if he was trying to ape the Stalinist style or if he was simply expressing his own version of the lantern-jawed, blue-collar worker. Given the title of the installation, he's probably leaning (ironically or not) toward the former option.

Regardless, at more than 10 feet tall, the stoic duo are quite an impressive sight. As they proudly display the core items of their chosen trade, you can't help but wonder what such a magnificent specimen of welded manhood might be holding in front of a lingerie store . . .

Pomeroy has several other pieces on public display in and around Billings, including *Bear*, at the Student Center of Rocky Mountain College, 1511 Poly Drive; *Football Player No. 41*, at Winners Circle Sports Bar on 2501 Grand Avenue; *Sheraton Coat of Arms*, at 1600 Avenue East; *Hitching Post*, in the lounge of Logan International Airport; and *Sir Speedy*, at Roscoe Steel on 2847 Hesper Road.

The *Statues for the Proletariat* can be seen at 1144 Broadwater Avenue in Billings.

She Sells Sea Shells, Nowhere Near the Sea Shore
Broadus

Mac McCurdy washed out in his first attempt at building a life in Montana. Not able to make it as a farmer, he hightailed it back to Delaware where he developed a passion for collecting seashells.

When he finally did return to his beloved Big Sky state, he brought with him one of the most extensive seashell collections you'll see this side of the Gulf Coast. They're on display in the Powder River

★ ★

Historical Museum in Broadus. Each shell has been meticulously catalogued and identified with a hand-typed tag. The collection is displayed in handsome wood and glass cases that were built by students in the local high school.

According to museum curator Pam Ware, Mac had a special relationship with the kids in Broadus, and he wanted to make sure every child had at least one real seashell. Kids would gather at the shell museum, and he'd bury shells in a box of sand. The youngsters would then do some landlocked beachcombing, digging through the sand to find the shells.

The collection also includes a small assortment of robin's eggs, some from as far back as 1904. These tiny blue eggs first ignited Mac's interest in collecting specimens from nature. He also enjoyed

At the Powder River Historical Museum, the smell of low tide mixed with a nearby barnyard can be intoxicating.

collecting arrowheads and butterflies, many of which are on display here as well.

But it's the seashells that are the main attraction. From conchs to whelks to huge abalones, Mac's collection is amazing in its breadth. According to Ware, even people from Sanibel, Florida (widely considered a seashell-collecting Mecca), are suitably impressed when they visit this massive collection, 1,100 miles from the nearest ocean.

The Powder River Historical Museum in Broadus stands at the crossroads of MT 59 and US 212. Call (406) 436-2753 for more information. If you hold the phone up to your ear just right, you might hear the ocean.

It's in a School, But It's Way Cool
Colstrip

The Schoolhouse History and Art Center in Colstrip is, indeed, located in an old schoolhouse, a roomy, cross-shaped building years removed from its days of math quizzes and spelling bees. One exhibit is permanent, telling the story of Colstrip in a series of historic, black-and-white photos. In a larger room toward the back, there are several paintings by local artists. The room is hung with a new show every couple of months. Several couches and overstuffed chairs provide a comfy place to hang out; you can sit back and stroke your chin while you view the paintings, giving the impression that you know something about art.

The little gift shop off to the side is full of whimsical treasures created by local artists and craftspeople. Prices are reasonable, and you'll definitely find something unique to take home.

The center also offers art classes in subjects that range from pottery to drawing to jewelry making.

The Schoolhouse History and Art Center is located at 400 Woodrose Street in Colstrip. Call (406) 748-4822 for more information.

★ ★

A Dinosaur to Call Their Very Own

Glendive

In an area famous for its wealth of dinosaur fossils, the intrepid paleontologist might think he's seen it all. From a *Diplodocus* to a duck-
billed *Hadrosaur* to the Elvis Presley of dinosaurs, the T-rex, all sorts
of dino bones have been unearthed in Montana's Great Plains.

But there's been only one known specimen of the fearsome
Glendisaurus. It dates back to the Holocene era (circa, last week)
and stands 30 feet long and 14 feet tall. A sculpture based on *Triceratops*, it's actually the brainchild of Joe Crisafulli and Len Watson

Don't call her fat; she's just big-boned.

★ ★

Trivia

Theodore Roosevelt was a charter member of the Montana Stock Growers Association. Bully for him.

of Glendive. It's kind of a stylized version, though, looking like it was designed by the same people who came up with Gumby and Pokey.

Glenda, as she's called, keeps a watchful eye on MT 16 from her spot at the edge of Hollecker Lake. She appears to be constructed of stucco or plaster over a fiberglass shell. Her eyes are light sockets and, when they're working, probably lend a frightening element to the rough-skinned creature.

A plaque in front of the *Glendisaurus* explains that she was "spearheaded" by Craig Hostetler and Dan Bushnell. If you're coming in or out of Glendive on MT 16, she's hard to miss. Look for Olmstead Lane just north of Glendive.

Custer's Last Stand, Every Year
Hardin

While the rest of the country was getting ready for its centennial celebration, Gen. George Armstrong Custer and the 7th Cavalry were hauling a Gatling gun around eastern Montana, looking for trouble. As we all learned in third grade history, they found it.

Historians differ as to the actual number of combatants (none of Custer's men survived to tell the tale) at the Battle of Little Bighorn, but most agree that around 1,800 Lakota Sioux and Northern Cheyenne killed nearly all of the 300 U.S. Cavalry soldiers on the rolling bluffs near what is now Crow Agency.

★ ★

Custer's Last Stand has also become known as the Battle of Little Bighorn, presumably to shift the spotlight off the losing team. The 1876 battle was a watershed event in U.S. history, and you can relive the bloody conflict every summer just a few miles from the spot where General Custer uttered his last "What the . . . ?"

The Custer's Last Stand Reenactment takes place in late June of each year, 6 miles west of Hardin. The Battle of Little Bighorn is staged from a script written by Crow tribal historian Joe Medicine Crow, and tells the story from the Indian perspective.

For a complete picture, you can also visit the Little Bighorn Battlefield National Monument in Crow Agency, where both Indian and U.S. Cavalry warriors are memorialized.

For reenactment dates and directions, visit the Custer's Last Stand Reenactment Web site at www.custerslaststand.org.

How the West Was Watered
Huntley

Montana has its share of museums (over 200 at last count). No matter your inclinations and interests, and considering the wide-ranging history of America's fourth-largest state, you can almost be sure to find one that piques your interest.

The Huntley Project Museum of Irrigated Agriculture is right near the top of the list of museums with the longest name. Located just a few miles east of Billings, the HPMIA is a vital and unique establishment that tells the story of the homesteaders who transformed the once-arid valley into lush and fertile farmland.

If you're thinking endless examples of lawn sprinklers, you're way off. It's the only museum of its kind in Montana, and you'll find vast amounts of information and history unavailable anywhere else. You'll be pleasantly surprised by the incredible depth to this historical collection. Plan to spend at least half of a day.

Some eighteen homestead-era buildings make up the museum complex, and each is loaded with collections of tools, artifacts, machinery, and all manner of items that will make you feel like you've stepped back in time.

In addition to the main house, there's a granary, a garage, a chicken coop, a corncrib, and a Russian-style barn. It's easy to picture the hardscrabble life endured by pioneers as they tried to carve out a place for themselves in this harsh, unforgiving part of the country.

You can walk down "Main Street" and be transported in time as you pass Dr. DeMers's Office, the First National Bank of Pompeys Pillar, the Osborne Mercantile, and other faithfully restored buildings.

Well, the world needs ditch diggers, too. Machines.
Ditch-digging machines.

★ ★

Farming machinery plays a big part in the museum. There are tractors and haymakers, a McCormick thresher, and a massive machine called a Ruth Dredger (parked just yards away from the irrigation ditch it helped dig out of the earth).

Several special events take place during the summer, details of which can be seen on the museum's educational, informative Web site.

The Huntley Project Museum of Irrigated Agriculture is close to the juncture of Eighth Road and US 312, near Huntley. Give them a ring at (406) 348-2533 or visit their Web site at www.huntleyproject museum.org.

Hey, Cowboy—Get Off My Back
Miles City

Imagine if you were to go to a cattle auction, but before you plunked down a couple grand for a cow, you wanted to see how the hamburger tasted. That's kind of the idea at Miles City's famous Bucking Horse Sale.

Held the third weekend in May each year, the Bucking Horse Sale is kind of a Bronc-a-palooza for the Stetson set. Rodeo stock contractors come from all over North America to see bucking broncos in action, so they can pick the best of the bunch to appear in rodeos and exhibitions all over the world.

But the Bucking Horse Sale is so much more than a simple "try before you buy" auction. The population of Miles City swells to more than double its size over the weekend, as rodeo fans, horse racing enthusiasts, and weekend cowpokes of all types gather for the festival that helps usher in the Montana summer season.

There are art shows, horse racing (both pari-mutuel and the wild variety), live bands, barbecues and street dances, and all kinds of cultural events to keep folks entertained all weekend long. Cowboy hats are not required, but pardner, it sure wouldn't hurt.

I reckon if you want the lowdown on the Bucking Horse Sale, you can drift on over to their Web site: www.buckinghorsesale.com.

★ ★

Trivia

The largest snowflake ever recorded, according to the Guinness Book of World Records, was observed in Fort Keogh, and measured 15 inches across. Can you imagine having to shovel your driveway one flake at a time?

The Pioneer Museum That Has Everything
Miles City

What is quite possibly the most extensive and eclectic pioneer museum in Montana is actually seven museums in one.

It's known collectively at the Range Riders Museum, and their sheer volume of treasures and relics from Montana's past is mind-boggling. This is far more than just a permanent yard sale full of a bunch of junk found in Grandpa's barn; it's seven buildings' worth of pioneer history. The displays of weaponry in the Bert Clark gun collection, the photos and stories of the pioneers in the Range Riders Memorial Hall, and even the fashions and uniforms in the Coach House will keep you fascinated for hours.

There are the predictable buffalo skulls, Indian war bonnets, muzzle-loader rifles and old farm tools, but the museum is also full of surprises. There are bagpipes, ladies hats, a 1918 Model T Ford, and an entire wing dedicated to nurses. It's like they couldn't decide on what angle of the West would be their focus so they said, what the heck—let's include everything!

The Vehicle Barn is pretty interesting, with the aforementioned Model T displayed alongside a fully restored 1917 Dodge. There are also stages and chuck wagons and wagons for carrying grain and freight.

The museum sits on the original site of Fort Keogh. This is reflected in the Officers Quarters building, which is a faithful re-creation of a military man's home. Each room is outfitted according to the period, right down to the cloth napkins on the dining table.

Inside the Coach House you'll find three huge dioramas: the Fort Keogh scene, the now-defunct Lame Deer Ranch, and a detailed depiction of Chief Lame Deer's original camp (Lame Deer was killed in a skirmish with U. S. troops shortly after the Battle of Little Big-horn). The backgrounds are expertly painted, and the dioramas blends seamlessly into the walls around them.

Don't go through Miles City without making a stop at the Range Riders Museum. Ask a volunteer for a tour, and make sure you have plenty of time. You'll soak up a ton of early Montana history.

The Range Riders Museum is located at 443 I-94 Business Loop in Miles City. Call (406) 232-6146 to enter the equivalent of a time warp.

Way Better Than Writing His Name in the Snow
Pompeys Pillar

It's not exactly a hidden gem—it's a national monument, for crying out loud—but Pompeys Pillar, 25 miles east of Billings, is definitely worth a peek if you're traveling through that part of the state. Where else can you see Capt. William Clark's signature?

Creating what may be Montana's first documented case of White Explorer's Graffiti, Clark carved his name and the date (July 25, 1806) into the soft sandstone of a huge rock outcropping near the Yellowstone River. As the story goes, he had climbed to the top of the butte, which is as big as your average Holiday Inn Express, to gain a view of the area during his return trip from the Pacific coast. There were no boxcars nearby to spray paint, so he decided to tag the rock instead. His signature, now protected by a brass and glass case, is the only remaining physical evidence of the Lewis and Clark Expedition.

The name for the rock pillar comes from Clark's nickname for Sacagawea's baby boy, whom he called "Pomp." The rock's original

★ ★

"Kilroy Was Here" was already taken.

name, "Pompy's Tower," was later changed to "Pompeys Pillar," by Nicholas Biddle, first editor of the Lewis and Clark journals.

A boardwalk leads to Captain Clark's signature and to the top of the pillar, and several walking trails run past a replica of Clark's canoes and to a view of the Yellowstone River. At the signature site, dozens of other signatures are also visible, having been carved into the rock over the years by disrespectful wisenheimers. The practice is now forbidden, however, and may be punishable by years of bad juju.

In November 1991 the historic landmark was purchased from private ownership. Pompeys Pillar National Monument was created in 2001 and placed under the management of the Secretary of the Interior through the Bureau of Land Management.

Pompeys Pillar National Monument is easily accessible from I-94 on exit 23, or from US 312. The park is open from April 30 until October 15, and the landmark is open to walk-in visitation during the off-season.

Mystery Stones Suggest Lewis and Clark Were Not Here First
Wibaux

In an old train car behind the Wibaux House museum, you'll find all kinds of relics from the pioneer days: old photos, cameras, rifles, currency, and even a vintage slot machine. But in a glass display case on the left, you'll see some items that will put a thread of doubt into everything you've learned about Lewis and Clark.

The Mystery Stones, as they're known, were unearthed in 1956 on the Leslie Baird farm, 4 miles northeast of Wibaux. Etched on these stones are the names of several people, some with apparent dates of death as well as a few cryptic symbols resembling crosses. The stones were all found near a lake. There was water, and plenty of good grass and game—the perfect location for an early group of settlers. But the dates on these stones, if they're to be believed, place the settlers in the area as much as fifteen years before Lewis and Clark came through on their first expedition.

Who the heck were these people? There is no written record other than these curious stones. Are they the modest grave markers of people killed in an Indian raid? Are they some primitive version of Facebook? No one knows.

Museum employee Lisa Kiedrowski told me that it's her understanding that the stones were sent to the Smithsonian Institute for verification around 2004, and they are believed to be legitimate. Other stones similar to these have been found near Miles City,

Was it all just an elaborate practical joke pulled
by Sacagawea on Lewis and Clark?

Ekalaka, and Sundance, Wyoming. The earliest date carved into
one of the Wibaux stones is 1790, and it's placed next to the name
of James Mead. What happened to the people who survived long
enough to carve these stones? Did they give up, say to heck with it,
and move north into Canada to take advantage of universal health
care? There are no answers. Only stones.

The Centennial Car Museum is just behind the Wibaux House at
the end of Orgain Avenue in Wibaux.

★ ★

The Church of Rock
Wibaux

No, it's not a sequel to the *School of Rock*, although even Jack Black would be impressed with the sheer . . . . *rockness* of St. Peter's Catholic Church in Wibaux.

The church, which is listed in the National Register of Historic Places, was built in 1895 by R. R. Cummings and Eugene Blias of Glendive, at the request of town-founder Pierre Wibaux. Wibaux's father, Achille, apparently was dismayed that his son didn't have a proper Catholic church in his town, and sent his son $2,000 and instructions to build one. Like Black's character in *School of Rock*, Pierre lifted his goblet of rock and construction began.

At the time, the Wibaux congregation was a mission of Miles City, so Father Van der Brock of that town supervised the construction of the wood-framed building, which was designed in the Gothic Revival style.

In 1938 the church was enlarged, and that's when its exterior was covered in scoria, the rough and colorful volcanic rock common to the badlands of the Wibaux area. It was Father Leahy, pastor of the church beginning in 1931, who first said, "Let there be rock." Volunteers from the congregation went on rock-picking expeditions, loading the gnarly stuff into wagons and pickup trucks to bring back to town. And it was good.

The building served as Wibaux's Catholic church until 1965, when a new church was built and this one was converted into a catechism school. That was when it did indeed become the School of Rock.

St. Peter's Catholic Church is on the corner of Orgain Avenue West and C Street South in Wibaux.

In Wibaux, a Man Named Wibaux Who Loved Wibaux

The urge to give your name to a place you discover runs deep in men, especially the men who swarmed across the West in the 1800s, wiping out Native American tribes and claiming the land for their own. Pierre Wibaux, for instance, a particularly arrogant rancher, apparently arranged to have a town named after him.

Wibaux emigrated from France in 1884, and was in the right place at the right time when the harsh winter of 1886–87 wiped out many of the cattle ranches in eastern Montana. Wibaux shrewdly bought up the remaining stock from ranchers who were ready to throw in the bandana, and by the early 1890s his herd numbered more than 75,000 head.

According to legend, Wibaux was drunk with power (and possibly whiskey) when he had his cowboys surround the little town of Mingusville. They wouldn't let anyone in or out until the residents had signed a petition changing the name of the town to Wibaux.

Wibaux also had a church built and named after him, and put his moniker on Wibaux County. He celebrated his achievements by having a statue of himself erected on a hill overlooking town. His likeness stands atop a rough granite block, holding a rifle and a pair of binoculars, presumably so he can scan the horizon looking for something else he can name after himself.

The statue of Pierre Wibaux is on G Street South and Orgain Avenue West, just south of the train tracks in Wibaux.

Well, it certainly gives it that "prayed in" look.

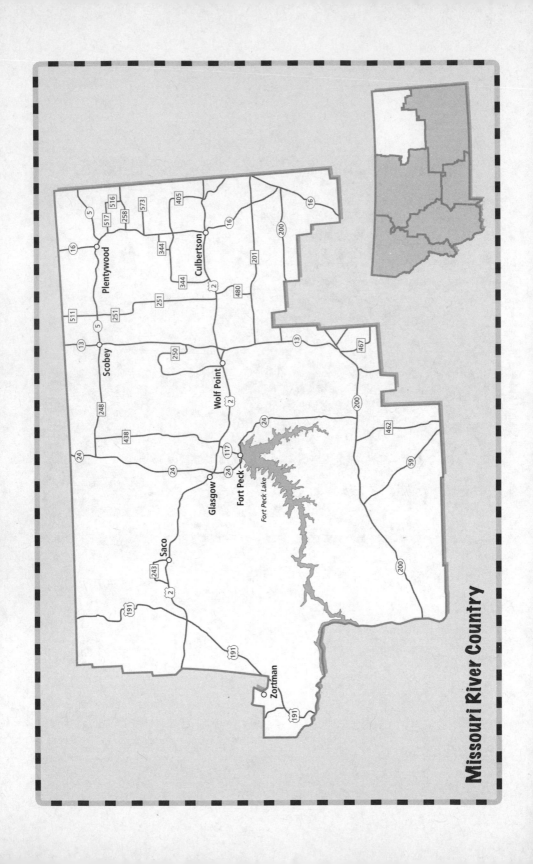

Missouri River Country

5

Missouri River Country

The rugged country in the northeast corner of Montana is laced with badlands and smeared with history. Kid Curry, the "wildest of the Wild Bunch," used to ride these parts between train heists and hanging out with Butch Cassidy and the Sundance Kid. The country's longest river, the Missouri, meanders through the Northern Plains, its murky waters home to the paddlefish, a butt-ugly creature that has been around for 65 million years.

Folks here are as friendly as anywhere, though, whether you're ordering by phone from your table at the Old Town Grill in Wolf Point or plugging coins into the lone parking meter in the border town of Glentana.

It's true, though, that the area's harsh winters and barren landscape can help bring out the crazy in a person. Maybe that's what happened to the hobo who filled the walls inside an abandoned caboose with Bible scripture and lurid drawings. And what was going through the minds of the Freemen of Jordan when they barricaded themselves away from the FBI? Maybe they were receiving signals from Smoky Butte, where amalcolite is found. There are only three other places where you can find that stuff: the Ukraine, South Africa, and the moon.

And who knows? Amalcolite might also help explain why a man in Glasgow felt compelled to embed a "crashed" airplane into the side of his bar.

For whatever the reason, some of Montana's wildest and most interesting curiosities are in Missouri River Country. Buckle up.

All Aboard the Hobo Art Caboose
Culbertson

It's cold. It's dark. You've got nothing to eat but a dented can of beans and the remains of a wadded-up Big Mac you found in a trash can. You haven't brushed your teeth since last winter and your pants are full of lice. You sit back in a musty, abandoned caboose and look around at the empty walls, wondering what's next.

For one hobo in Great Falls, the answer was art. The rust-colored, decommissioned Great Northern train caboose sat in the Great Falls rail yard for years. And for much of that time, it was inhabited by a homeless—but driven—man who had a lot to say, most of it from the Bible.

Using felt markers, the pontificating drifter methodically covered nearly every square inch of the walls inside the caboose with Bible quotes, melodramatic illustrations, and warnings of the Great Apocalypse. On one wall there's a life-size drawing of some kind of avenging knight outfitted for battle, done up in several colors. He wears a helmet emblazoned with the word, "SALVATION." He wields a sword that reads, "SPIRIT." His shield says, "FAITH," his belt reads, "TRUTH," and his shoes say, "ADIDAS."

Another masterpiece, on the side wall, is the *First Rider of the Apocalypse*. It features someone identified as the "great whore" astride a seven-headed beast. It's enough to creep a guy out. The illustrations are done in a style that evokes the loopy, airbrushed scenery on the front of a carnival funhouse.

The caboose hobo's obsession is even more impressive when you realize that all the lettering is done in a serifed-style font, much of it set off with deftly rendered highlights. No one knows what became of this Bible-quoting bum, but one look around the inside of his erstwhile home makes it clear that he managed to get a lot off his chest while he was here.

The Hobo Art Caboose now rests in the fenced yard of the Culbertson Museum and Visitor Center on US 2 in Culbertson. Call (406) 787-6320 or visit www.culbertsonmt.com.

I know he's a penniless hobo, but could somebody
give this guy a sketch pad?

★ ★

Trivia

In 1925 the town of Scobey hired blacklisted baseball players from the Chicago Black Socks to help them beat the Plentywood team. The game was so lopsided that for a while afterwards the town was known as NotSoMuchwood.

That's a Lot of Dam Dirt
Fort Peck

Like most kids, you might have carried buckets full of dirt down to your little backyard stream to make a dam. Do you remember how difficult it was to keep even the smallest flow from making its way downstream? Try to imagine making a dirt dam 4 miles long.

That's exactly what President Roosevelt did in 1933 when he proposed the Fort Peck Project, which included construction of the Fort Peck Dam. When it was completed, it was (at the time) the largest earth-filled dam in the world. The dam, which created the 134-mile-long Fort Peck Lake, was designed to provide hydroelectric power, flood control, and water quality management. Not to mention providing thousands of jobs at a time when the nation was in the grips of the Great Depression.

At 250 feet, the Fort Peck Dam is the highest of the six dams along the northern Missouri. The hydraulically filled dam is made up of clay and silt in its core, surrounded by a crunchy candy shell. Just kidding.

The numbers pertaining to the construction and size of the dam are staggering. Twenty thousand feet of 28-inch pipeline were used to carry dredged material to the dam site by the "Fort Peck Navy"—four dredging units that were built on-site. At the peak of construction work in 1936, some 10,546 people were working on the dam project. By the time it began generating electricity in 1943, the project had created more than a dozen small towns where the workers and their families lived.

It was not all beer and skittles, though. In 1938 part of the embankment slid into the reservoir, taking with it thirty-four men. All but eight were rescued. It was eventually determined that the likely cause of the slide was the low shear strength of the bentonite under the dam. The dam is now fortified by a cutoff wall, 34 million tons of steel thrust deep into the bentonite and shale beneath the dam. This is good news to the people living downstream.

Today Fort Peck Lake, in the Charles M. Russell National Wildlife Refuge, provides recreation for thousands of visitors each year. The dam currently generates up to 185,250 kilowatts of electricity. There's a great museum in the town of Fort Peck that tells the story of the dam. For more information, visit www.fortpeckdam.com.

No, It's Not Named After Marty Feldman
Fort Peck

In *Napoleon Dynamite*, the titular character tries to impress a girl at school by saying, "I caught you a delicious bass." The geeky high schooler would have stood a better chance of scoring if he had caught a walleye instead.

The popular northern game fish that looks like a cross between a bass and a trout is widely considered to be the tastiest of freshwater fish. It's the state fish of both Minnesota and South Dakota, but those states have nothing on Montana and its Rock Creek Walleye Tournament, held annually at Fort Peck Reservoir.

The oldest tournament of the Montana walleye circuit, the Fort Peck event draws over one hundred anglers each year, all hoping to go home with a winner's plaque and a photo of themselves holding a ten-pounder. The Rock Creek marina hosts the event in early June each year, and the catch-and-release format helps maintain a fishery that boasts walleye as big as those found in Lake Erie. Gosh!

When you're ready to wet your line, call tournament organizer Steve Harada at (406) 653-1463, or cast your mouse over to the Montana Walleyes Unlimited Web site at www.montanawalleyes unlimited.net.

This Skunk Would Make Pepe Le Pew Proud
Glasgow

Glasgow's Pioneer Museum of Valley County is a cavernous building stuffed full of cultural artifacts from the early days of the Hi-Line, a period when settlers and pioneers were flooding into the area to stake their claim on this wide-open frontier.

The Glasgow museum has one of the most eclectic collections you'll find, starting with a 30-foot-long Plesiosaur spine stretched out near the entrance. You can see an original C. M. Russell watercolor (*A Midsummer Night's Dream*), valued at around $36,000, just down the aisle from a letter written by J. Edgar Hoover. In the back of the museum there's a vintage back bar that contains a bullet hole purportedly put there by Buffalo Bill.

They also have an extremely rare sheep displayed near the entryway. It's a full-body mount of an Audubon sheep, an animal that became extinct in the early 1900s. This is one of only three full mounts in the whole state. There's also a head mount of the defunct species in a back-room display.

Some museums are lucky enough to have a two-headed calf. This museum has at least three. And there's also an albino black-tailed deer, a surprised-looking black bear, and an 18-foot-long boa constrictor skin. The taxidermy display has hundreds of mounts, ranging from raccoons to moose, and all kinds of western birds. And don't miss the 62.5-pound buffalo fish caught in nearby Fort Peck Lake. A placard reads, "Damn It, This Is No Carp."

One of the more peculiar mounts, though, is a bobcat that looks like he's performing some kind of unnatural act on a skunk. The

★ ★

panicked look on the cat's face just adds to the humorous effect, and the skunk seems resigned to his fate. I'm not sure this was the intention of the taxidermist, but it definitely makes for some interesting photo opportunities. Meow!

Glasgow's Pioneer Museum of Valley County is at 816 US 2. They're open seven days a week from Memorial Day to Labor Day. There is a one-time fee ($3 for adults, $2 for kids, and children under six are admitted for free).

Museum curators do not condone this sort of behavior, but hope that this mount serves as a warning to skunks everywhere.

More Dinosaurs Than a Classic Rock Radio Station

From the Two Medicine Dinosaur Center in Bynum to the Carter County Museum in Ekalaka, the eastern two-thirds of Montana is a veritable treasure trove of dinosaur fossils and exhibits. Once you get out of the mountains of the northern Rockies and move into the plains and badlands, you're in prime dino territory. In fact, there is a Dinosaur Trail that loosely connects more than a dozen important sites and museums throughout the state.

Amateur paleontologists and seasoned scientists alike will find plenty to see. The "trail" covers a good portion of the state, but you can see more than half of the exhibits if you travel along the Hi-Line, on U.S. Highway 2. Public education programs and even guided tours of dig sites will show you why Montana is one of the most important states in the hunt for information about these scaly giants that once roamed the earth. And by that I mean the dinosaurs, not Fleetwood Mac.

Dig up some more information by visiting http://mtdinotrail .org.

★ ★

"Sir, That's Not a Drive-Thru"
Glasgow

As you head east out of Glasgow, keep your eyes on the road along
US 2. Do not be distracted, even if you think you see the unlikely
sight of a small airplane embedded in the side of a bar.

Because you do. And it is. The Piper Cub that seems to have become
one with the Hangar Bar was actually put there on purpose by the bar's
aviation-loving owner, Jerry Koski. He likes flying so much, in fact, that
he bought the bar (formerly known as the Roost) and completely rede-
signed the interior to mimic the shape of an airplane.

"You can forget a lot of problems when you're flying," says Koski,
explaining why aviation appeals to him. He'd bought the Piper Cub
for a song after it was damaged by a "mini tornado" that came
through the area and tossed the craft onto a rock pile. He and some
friends slaved away, pounding out the dents and replacing sections
until they got the Cub back to presentable shape. Then, because he
thought it would look cool, they attached it to the side of the bar in
such a way that it would look like it had flown right into the building.

Koski is currently making plans to put the motor and prop on the
inside wall to complete the illusion.

Glasgow's Hangar Bar is at 54315 US 2 East. Call (406) 228-8280
to book a flight.

Huntley Schoolhouse Restored, Film at Eleven
Saco

If you're old enough to remember Chet Huntley, you might be surprised to know that the venerable newsman was born and raised in
eastern Montana. Huntley's father was a Northern Pacific Railroad
telegraph operator, and his job took his family all over the area, from
Cardwell (Chet was born in the depot's living quarters) to Saco, and
from Willow Creek to Three Forks. It's a wonder he ever bothered to
unpack his suitcase.

This is where Chet Huntley began his
journalism education.

Huntley was, of course, the serious half of the pioneering news team of Huntley and Brinkley. The duo's popularity came from the obvious on-camera chemistry between the deadpan Huntley and the sharp-witted David Brinkley. The *Huntley-Brinkley Report* began airing on NBC in October of 1956, with the news hounds covering the Presidential election. Their trademark sign-off ("Good night, Chet."/ "Good night, David, and good night from NBC News.") became a famous phrase in the popular lexicon, right up there with Vinnie Barbarino's pithy, "Up your nose with a rubber hose," from *Welcome Back Kotter*.

The town of Saco claims Huntley as their favorite son, and the Saco Garden Club has restored the original schoolhouse where he spent several years behind a desk. The Huntley School is open for tours in the summer. The one-room schoolhouse is chock full of vintage furniture and schoolroom paraphernalia from the early twentieth century. The old iron and wood desks all have an inkwell hole, and a potbelly stove sits in the center of the room. Up front, flanking the chalkboard, are the obligatory framed pictures of George Washington and Abraham Lincoln.

It's interesting to see the actual roots of the education that helped shape one of professional journalism's most revered figures. Huntley made his last broadcast in 1970 and retired to Montana, where he established the Big Sky Ski Resort. He passed away in Big Sky in 1973. Good night, Chet.

The Huntley School is on US 2, on the east edge of Saco.

It's a Good Thing They Like Green
Wolf Point

John Deere buffs, your Valhalla awaits. In a large warehouse just north of Wolf Point, you can walk among the largest collection of John Deere tractors in the world.

You'll feel like you've died and gone to the farm when you look out over the sea of green machines. The main warehouse holds over

Did you hear about the farmer's wife who left him?
She sent him a John Deere letter.

200 specimens, and another 300 or so are stashed throughout the property in various outbuildings. This Holy Grail of the agriculture set is the work of Wolf Point resident Louis Toavs.

Toavs passed away a few years back, but his son-in-law John Jackson picked up the gearshift and now keeps the museum humming. Jackson and his assistants travel quite a bit, taking restored tractors to shows and exhibitions, sometimes coming back to their Wolf Point headquarters with a new prize in the trailer they pull behind their ginormous motor home.

The collection is overwhelming in its size and completeness. There is a D-series tractor from every year they were made. They also have at least one of every kind of two-cylinder tractor made by John Deere, up to the last one, which rolled off the line in 1967. The tractors are in various stages of restoration. Some gleam like they're back in the showroom while others are "still wearing their work clothes," as Jackson likes to say.

There are stationary engines—minus wheels of course—alongside general purpose A and B models, and a few industrial-use tractors, which are painted an incongruous yellow. Those tractors stick out in the sea of green like goldfish in a bucket of frogs.

Trivia

Fort Peck Lake has 1,520 miles of shoreline—the same as the coast of California. Only the surfing at Fort Peck Lake isn't quite as good.

★ ★

Adjacent to the main warehouse is a small room stuffed with hundreds of John Deere models and toys. Overhead, the room is ringed with a few decades' worth of John Deere hats. There's also an incredibly detailed diorama that depicts a farming operation from the days before the arrival of the John Deere tractor. Those little tiny guys look like they're doing everything the hard way.

Two impressive pieces are a pair of machined tractor models (⅜ scale and ¼ scale) that actually run. These machines should come in handy if they ever decide to plant corn in Munchkinland.

Louis Toavs's John Deere tractor collection is 15 miles north of Wolf Point on MT 250. Tours are available by appointment. Their phone number is (406) 392-5294.

Do They Use Caller I.D. to Find Your Table?
Wolf Point

The Old Town Grill in Wolf Point looks like an old-school drive-in that moved everybody inside. There's one feature of the old drive-in that they kept, though, and it makes for a pretty funny dining experience.

"Hello, I'd like to order lunch," you say into the telephone at your table. The waitress talking with you on the other end is about 15 feet away. Kind of makes the whole exercise pointless, but that's part of the charm.

"Yeah, it's saved us a few million dollars in waitress costs," cracks Jerry, the head cook. The restaurant opened in 1981. The owners installed phones at each table as a nod to the old A&W drive-ins of the 1950s and '60s. Sure, it's a little silly, but it's also just the kind of goofy fun that breaks up the monotony of a drive along the Hi-Line. And the mushroom-and-Swiss burger is not too bad, either.

Wolf Point's Old Town Grill is located at 400 US 2 West. They can be reached by calling (406) 653-1031.

"Yeah, toots, I'd like the apple pie à la mode. And can you put a scoop of ice cream on that?"

★ ★

There's Gold at That Thar Motel

Zortman

"Welcome to Zortman—the Friendliest Little Town In Montana," reads the legend on the wooden bench outside the office of the Zortman Garage and Motel. In fact, the town is so friendly, they might let you leave with a pocketful of gold.

Zortman Garage, here since 1979, offers gold panning lessons, free of charge if you're a guest of the fifty-room motel. Owner John Kalal has set up containers of water in front of the motel, flat reservoirs where he can show potential millionaires how to swirl piles of dirt, sand, and rock around in ridged pans, slowly separating gold from sand, allowing the heavier flakes and dust (and hopefully nuggets) to settle behind the ridges. Once tourists get the hang of it, Kalal points them toward nearby Alder Gulch, where a productive gold mine was in operation from 1979 to 1998. It's still producing, although now most of its output is the gold powder known as flour gold.

Kalal brings truckloads of material down from the gulch to load the panning boxes, and visitors are generally successful in turning up at least a few small flakes of the shiny stuff. It's not uncommon to discover an occasional nugget in the process, and one panner recently found a chunk the size of a thumbnail. With the price of gold hovering around $1,000 an ounce, a nugget that size could pay for quite a few nights at the Zortman Motel, allowing a neo–gold panner to spend plenty of time out there in the gulch, looking for the next strike.

Zortman Garage and Motel is just past the Miner's Club Bar on the main road into town. Call (406) 673-3160 to stake a claim.

You're looking at some actual gold nuggets
panned from nearby Alder Gulch.

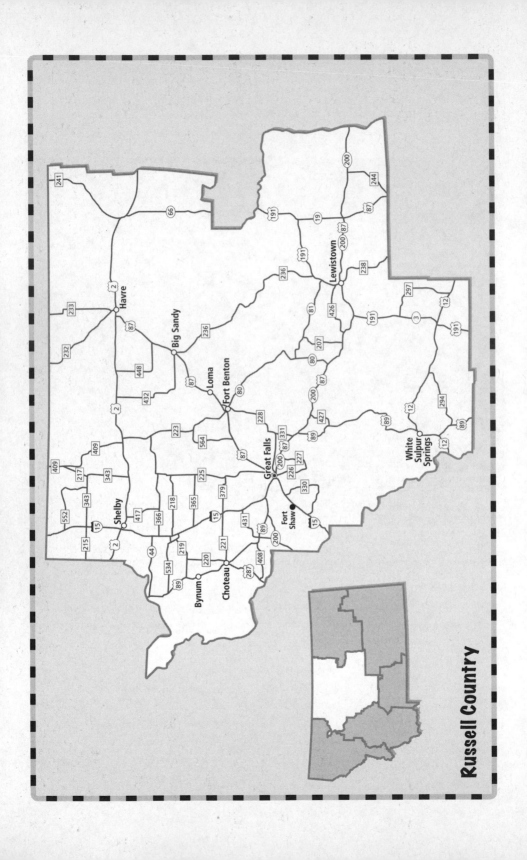

Russell Country

6

Russell Country

You'll find it *all, from large to small, in Russell Country. From the world's shortest river to a 375,000-acre national monument, the upper-middle chunk of Montana boasts an extraordinary variety of people, places, and things.*

Zip over to the airport and check out the world's largest model airplane collection, and even view a letter from Charles Lindbergh. Stop by the Holiday Village Mall where you can satisfy your inner cop by visiting the Law Enforcement Museum, then head south to take a tour of the Castle in White Sulphur Springs.

Weird history and strange monuments abound, especially in Fort Benton, once known as the country's most inland port. There you'll find the grave of Shep the faithful dog, and the oldest building in the state (maybe). If you've ever seen a buffalo nickel, you can see the beast that modeled for that coin at the museum. Just follow the buffalo tracks in the street.

The Streets Beneath Havre tour is a fascinating and odd glimpse into the subterranean history of that Hi-Line city. The farming community of Big Sandy is the hometown of both Montana senator Jon Tester and Pearl Jam bassist Jeff Ament. In the 1920s another celebrity, prize-fighter Jack Dempsey, helped achieve the near ruin of a little oil town. Learn all about that debacle at Shelby's Marias Museum.

Any way you cover it, Russell Country has a bounty of curiosities and roadside attractions, and the intrepid quirk-seeker will find plenty of ways to satisfy his inner inquisitiveness.

World's Longest Dinosaur Still Extinct
Bynum

How do you fit a 137-foot dinosaur into a 60-foot building? You'll just have to visit the Two Medicine Dinosaur Center in Bynum to see for yourself. The center is home to the world's largest, full-size skeletal model of a dinosaur. Mostly neck and tail, the *Seismosaurus* (literally, earth-shaking lizard) stands 23 feet tall at the hip.

Actually, the *Seismosaurus* is a super-size version of the *Diplodocus*, one of the more commonly found dinosaur species in Montana. This whopper, though, is so long and so tall that it doubles back on itself a couple of times just to fit into the cavernous building that houses the center.

There are also several other fossils and displays to see, of course, including a 5.5 ton, 11-foot block containing fragments and bones of three individuals and two separate species. But it's the big bony guy that easily dominates the room.

According to resident paleontologist David Trexler, the original, fossilized bones of the *Seismosaurus* were found in 1979 by a couple hikers in what is today the Ojito Wilderness area, near Albuquerque. Official excavation was finally started in 1985, and experts were able to extrapolate the beast's size by comparing the bones to those of *Diplodocus*. The size estimations have been tweaked over the years, but finally a full-size replica was created. The individual bones were carved out of Styrofoam and wrapped in a harder "skin."

Five thousand people a year come through the center to gape up at the skeleton, says Trexler. Several hundred sign on for a day-long "how-to" session, where they learn the basic skills needed to search and excavate fossils.

"There are fewer than one hundred degreed paleontologists in this country," says Trexler, "and there are millions of acres of land to explore." Maybe one day someone who was trained at the Two Medicine Dinosaur Center may unearth a new species even bigger than the *Seismosaurus*. But they're going to need a bigger warehouse.

The Two Medicine Dinosaur Center is located on US 89 in Bynum. They're open year-round. From Memorial Day to Labor Day, they're open from 9 a.m. to 5 p.m. Their winter hours vary, depending on how snowbound they are. Call (800) 238-6873 or visit www.tm dinosaur.org.

A Case of Overkill
Choteau

Frontier life in Montana was pretty rough, and tempers were always a little short. A guy could easily rub people the wrong way. But in the Old Trail Museum in Choteau, you can look at the skeleton of a guy who must have royally teed somebody off.

Old Sol, as he is known, is the only skeleton known to have a Hudson's Bay Company arrowhead embedded in his bones. Four arrowheads, in fact: two in the back, one in the hip, and one in the breastbone. Experts who reassembled the skeleton, which was found in eastern Montana in the 1930s, say the arrowhead locations indicate that he was shot from at least two different directions. Hmm. Wrong place at the wrong time?

There was probably more to it than that—his skull was pierced by a bullet, and also shattered by a tomahawk. Wow. Did he refuse to wipe his feet when he stepped into someone's tipi? Was he a cable guy who kept someone waiting for hours before installing HBO at their trading post? Nobody knows.

The bones were found in a shallow grave near Circle, and plans were made to display the remains in a local library. But then Old Sol disappeared for fifty years, only to resurface in Great Falls. Scientists determined that he was probably a European male, thirty-five to forty years old, with an objectionable personality. Was he a trapper who never picked up the check? A settler who drank milk straight from the teat? A pioneer who never replaced the toilet paper roll? All we know for sure is that someone was royally torqued off at this guy, and wanted him dead in the worst way.

★ ★

You can view Old Sol up close and personal at the museum, but don't miss the other interesting displays, including the story of the last man hanged in Choteau, in 1933. In light of Old Sol's fate, I'm surprised that guy wasn't poisoned, hanged, and then put in the electric chair in front of a firing squad.

The Old Trail Museum is located at 823 North Main Street in Choteau, open during the summer months. Be nice to them when you call, (406) 466-5332 or visit their Web site, www.theoldtrailmuseum.org.

Old Shep, the World's Most Faithful Dog
Fort Benton

If ever a dog deserved an extra Milk Bone or two, it would have been Old Shep, the "ever faithful" pride of Fort Benton.

Of course, Fort Benton has lots to offer besides the grave of Old Shep. There's the Grand Union Hotel, the official Lewis and Clark Memorial, the Museum of the Northern Great Plains, and what is billed as the oldest standing building in Montana. But it's the grave of Old Shep, and his magnificent riverside monument, that seems to attract a consistent stream of dog-loving visitors.

The story is a true one, and it had a nation gratefully distracted from the distress of the Great Depression when it was broadcast on the radio in the 1930s. People loved hearing about the unwavering mission of Old Shep, the sheepdog who maintained a vigil at the train station in Fort Benton, meeting all four trains each day to look for his owner, a sheepherder, to debark. What Shep didn't understand was that the man had died in a Fort Benton hospital in August of 1935, and his body was sent back East to relatives.

But Shep never gave up hope. Every day for the next five and a half years, the persistent pooch went out to the tracks to meet the trains. His story gained national notoriety, and people across the land sent cards, gifts, and offers of adoption, touched by the dog's loyalty and hopefulness.

★ ★

Call him all you want. He's not going to come.

In January of 1942 Shep's vigil came to an end. Old, weak, and deaf, he failed to hear the approach of the 10:17, and slipped on an icy rail trying to escape its path. He was struck and killed. His funeral attracted hundreds of people, and he was buried on the hilltop overlooking the train station. His name is spelled out in bright yellow letters, and a life-size replica marks the spot.

In 1994 the townspeople commissioned Montana sculptor Bob Scriver to create a larger-than-life bronze statue of Shep. The faithful dog's likeness stands proudly, alert, one foot up on the railroad track, in the riverside park right next to the 130-year-old Grand Union Hotel (which, ironically, doesn't allow dogs), near St. Charles Street.

Renaissance Man in a Cowboy Hat

Guitar, bass, drums, harmonica, and accordion. It sounds like a pretty standard lineup for a country band, but when one man plays all the instruments simultaneously, it's a special kind of crazy. In this part of the West, it can be none other than Erik "Fingers" Ray, Montana's One-Man Band.

He sits down behind a bass drum, straps on one of his vintage, hollow-body electric guitars, and adjusts the harmonica in its neck holder. A squinty-eyed cowboy, he looks like he belongs in a Wild West gunfight, not onstage at some Montana roadhouse. Erik thumps the bass drum a couple of times, then launches into an energetic version of Hank Williams's "Honky Tonkin'." People begin to tap their feet and nod along with the music. This guy sounds better on his own than a lot of full bands. Soon dancers spill onto the dance floor . . . and another crowd has landed in the palm of Erik's hand.

Although he might be a weekend warrior, Erik is one of the best-known and most well-liked musicians in Montana. He started playing music professionally with a band in 1980, but by 1983 he'd grown tired of the politics and drama inherent in belonging to a group. "It just got too hard to hold a band together," he says. So the self-taught multi-instrumentalist struck out on his own and has been flying solo ever since.

"I've been playing every weekend for twenty-five years," he says. He still endures his share of drunks, honyockers, skinflint bar owners, and endless highway miles, "but once I get onstage, it's heaven," he says. After a gig, if he's more than 100 miles from his ranch in Conrad, he'll curl up in the back of his van under a buffalo robe to catch some Z's before heading home. "I know where all the best highway pullouts are," he says with a sly grin.

Once he gets back home after a weekend of entertaining crowds of barroom dancers, he hangs up his cowboy hat and grabs his textbooks. Erik has been teaching high school math in Conrad for over

The only bummer about being a one-man band is
that practice is always at your house.

twenty-five years, and plans to retire soon. After school, he puts the
cowboy hat back on and rides out onto his property where he runs a
cattle ranch.

Some days will find him up at dawn to feed the cattle, then it's off
to school to teach for seven hours. When the final bell rings, he hops
in his van to drive to some far-flung gig, where he'll play honky-tonk
music 'til 2 a.m., then drive home, collapse into bed, and grab two
hours of sleep before doing it all over again.

He wouldn't trade his life for anything, though, and thousands of
fans across the state are grateful for that.

For more information, visit www.myspace.com/erikfingersray.

★ ★

The Oldest Building in Montana. Probably.

Fort Benton

Established in 1846 as a trading post, the original Fort Benton is long gone, except for one single building, a block house that is the oldest standing building in Montana. The same claim is made, however, for the original Hudson's Bay Company trading post at Fort Connah, built in the same year. No one knows for sure which building is older, but one thing's for sure: Their plumbing systems are probably both shot.

As the fur-and-robe trading era wound down in 1865, the fort ("Gateway to the Missouri River") was sold to the military and became known, during the days of steamboat travel, as "The World's Most Inland Port." The discovery of gold in 1862 attracted a wild and transient population, giving Fort Benton ("The Birthplace of Montana") a reputation as a dangerous place for travelers. At one point the main thoroughfare was even called "The Bloodiest Street in the West."

Nowadays, the city of Fort Benton ("Town of a Hundred Nicknames") is a National Historic Site, crammed with monuments honoring this important crossroads of the American West. The Old Fort Benton monument is a great place to start.

In 1908 the Daughters of the American Revolution took on the task of restoring the crumbling remains of the fort. Archeological digs and historically accurate reconstructions of the adobe buildings have ensured that the Old Fort is a true replica of the original structure. The preservation effort is now maintained by the city, and by the nonprofit River and Plains Society.

Tours of the Old Fort are offered from late May to late September, for a small fee. That fee also gets you into the Museum of the Northern Great Plains, the Museum of the Upper Missouri, and the Upper Missouri Breaks Interpretive Center.

The fort is located in the Old Fort Park. The Fort Benton Chamber of Commerce is located at 1421 Front Street. Call (406) 622-3864 or rabble-rouse over to www.fortbenton.com.

He's Famous, But It Hasn't Gone to His Head
Fort Benton

When sculptor James Earl Fraser needed a model for his design of the buffalo nickel, he turned to Hornaday's Bull, the most famous buffalo in the world. You can see this impressive animal, standing guard over his family, at the Museum of the Northern Great Plains in Fort Benton.

Big Bull, as he's known, was killed and stuffed in 1886 by William T. Hornaday, "America's first taxidermist." Hornaday also killed and stuffed five other specimens in order to have a lasting representation of this proud species that was being decimated by white men who were, ahem, killing and stuffing them.

"Ooh, I couldn't eat another bite. I'm stuffed!"

★ ★

Trivia

Montana is the only state in the country where you can get legally married without actually showing up for the ceremony. I kid you not. Two designated proxies can stand in for the bride and the groom. Montana law requires at least one of the parties to be actively serving in the U.S. Military. Not having to rent a monkey suit? That's almost worth enlisting right there.

The irony of Hornaday's mission was not lost on him. "Under different circumstances," he wrote in his book, *The Extermination of the American Bison*, "nothing could have induced me to engage in such a mean, cruel, and utterly heartless enterprise." But he figured the bison were doomed. At least through his taxidermist's art, future Americans would know what they had lost. Millions of buffalo were wiped out by white men for their robes, for sport, and to drive the Plains Indians into submission by depriving them of their main source of food, clothing, and other essentials.

It was the Secretary of the Smithsonian Institute, Hornaday's employer, who ordered the zoologist to travel west to collect some specimens for preservation. After being shot near Miles City, the six bison were shipped to the Smithsonian where "The Group," as they were known, were expertly mounted and put on display. They remained there until 1955.

In addition to the buffalo nickel, Big Bull's image also was used for an edition of the ten dollar bill, and appears on the seal for the U.S. Department of Interior even today. The original group of bison was eventually moved to Fort Benton, whose residents raised the money for the transfer and restoration of the original mounts.

The Hornaday Buffalo are located at the Museum of the Northern

Great Plains in Fort Benton. From the monument of Old Fort Benton, follow the trail of huge yellow bison tracks down the street to 1205 Twentieth Street. Go to www.fortbenton.com/museums/ag.html for more information.

When Rez Ball Ruled the World
Fort Shaw

In the tiny Sun River Valley town of Fort Shaw, a monument stands in proud recognition of a small but poignant slice of Montana history. In 1903 over 300 Indian children from across America lived at the Fort Shaw Indian Boarding School. In the middle of this contentious time in America's westward expansion, nearly one hundred years before the WNBA, a small group of Indian girls took their basketball team to the very pinnacle of the sport, bringing home a trophy proclaiming them "Champions of the World."

Fred C. Campbell became administrator of the Indian school in 1898, and he was immediately impressed by the style of basketball played by the women's team. By 1902 he was scheduling inter-scholastic games with high school and college teams throughout Montana.

The team routinely mopped the hardwood floor with opposing squads, using an aggressive, turnover-producing style of play that would eventually be known as "rez ball." Superintendent Campbell, now the coach of the team, challenged the girls to meet their academic requirements, and the carrot he used to motivate them was a trip to the Louisiana Purchase Exposition in St. Louis in 1904.

The girls kept their end of the deal, and in June of 1904 the team boarded the train bound for the St. Louis World's Fair.

In St. Louis, the Montana girls lived with 150 other Indian children who were part of the fair's model Indian school exhibit. The team members, who came from Indian nations in Montana and Idaho, dealt with racial and gender stereotypes, but their talent and frenetic style of play began drawing large crowds of enthusiastic fans.

In honor of the 1904
Fort Shaw Indian Girls' Basketball Team

Standing from left: Seated from left:
Rose LaRose   Emma Sansaver
Flora Lucero   Genie Butch
Katie Snell   Belle Johnson
Minnie Burton
Genevieve Healy   Nettie Wirth
Sarah Mitchell

Dedicated in 2004 by the Sun River Valley Historical Society
And generations of descendants of the Fort Shaw Team.

They achieved the World's Championship without
a single shoe contract from Nike.

Toward the end of the exposition, the Indian team was challenged to a three-game series by a team of Missouri All-Stars. The winner would be named Champions of the World's Fair. People packed the stands to watch the outdoor games and cheered the Indian girls to victory over the Missouri All-Stars.

The Fort Shaw champions proudly brought the silver trophy home to Montana.

A PBS documentary, *Playing for the World*, was released in 2009. The film features interviews, photos, and archival footage to tell the story of this important chapter in Montana history. A novel, *Shoot, Minnie, Shoot*, is based on the story and is in development to be produced as a feature film.

The Fort Shaw 1904 World Championship Team monument is located at the entrance to Fort Shaw Elementary School, just south of the fire station.

This John's Big, But He Ain't So Bad
Great Falls

He's an outsize hombre you'd swear you've seen before. Perhaps you have. Big John has a few duplicates scattered throughout the country. One holds a muffler, one points to a great pancake restaurant, and the others, well, they're just kind of standing around.

They're known as the Muffler Men, named after the original that now resides in Wisconsin. Or maybe Massachusetts. They tend to be moved around every few years, to wherever a giant tin man may be needed to attract attention.

This particular Muffler Man represents a Great Falls casino, and his full-on western dress leaves no doubt that you're in cowboy country.

If you view the 20-foot-tall cowpoke from the side, there appears to also be no doubt as to his gender. But relax, that's just a thumb you see poking out. Big John, indeed.

Big John's Casino is located at 2323 Eleventh Avenue South in Great Falls. Call (406) 761-6077 to learn more.

He Must Have Been Flying Standby
Great Falls

In 1927 famed flyer Charles Lindbergh was scheduled to land in Great Falls during his barnstorming tour of America, but he ran short on time and had to cut the stop from his schedule. At least he was kind enough to drop a note. Literally.

Four months after his historic solo flight across the Atlantic, Lindbergh embarked on a promotional tour of the U.S., trying to drum up enthusiasm for "commercial aeronautics." Piloting the *Spirit of St. Louis,* Lindbergh crisscrossed the country, exhorting citizens to throw their support behind the growth of airmail, and the planning and building of a system of airports to accommodate the future of air travel.

When it was Great Falls' turn to welcome Lucky Lindy, though, he was already falling behind schedule and had to reduce his visit to a mere flyover. But what a flyover it was. Buzzing downtown Great Falls, Lindbergh flew just 50 feet over the rooftops, thrilling the crowd and acknowledging the gathered throng with a snappy salute. He also dropped a cloth bag that contained a signed form letter. In the letter, he thanked well-wishers, and asked for their continued support in the aeronautics movement.

The original letter—and even the cloth bag that held it—is displayed with little fanfare in the upstairs level of the Great Falls International Airport. According to the accompanying excerpt from a *Great Falls Tribune* account of the flyover, the falling letter struck a local woman on the shoulder before it tumbled to the sidewalk.

It's a small but thrilling episode in the history of Great Falls in the Roaring Twenties, and you can read all about it the next time you pass through the airport. As you look around and see the hundreds of travelers rushing to make their next flight, it might dawn on you that Lindy was right: Air travel was the key to our future.

The Great Falls International Airport is located 3 miles southwest of Great Falls, near the I-15/I-315 interchange.

Here's the best-kept secret of the Great
Falls Airport. Until now.

★ ★

In-Flight Movie? *Darby O'Gill and the Little People*
Great Falls

Montana may be sparsely populated, with just under a million souls inhabiting the U.S.'s fourth-largest state, but there's a place where you can go and see more airliners than you'd find at LAX during Spring Break. Most of these planes, though, are small enough to fit into your average overhead compartment.

Is That a Missile in Your Pasture, Or Are You Just Glad to Be Here?

At the height of the Cold War, some 200 Intercontinental Ballistic Missiles were hidden in silos beneath the ground throughout central Montana. Each missile, a Minuteman, contained a nuclear warhead. With a range of over 6,000 miles, these projectiles represented the U.S.'s greatest defense and deterrent to all-out nuclear war. With the diplomatic efforts of détente and the eventual collapse of the Soviet Union, many of these weapons were decommissioned, no longer needed to stand in America's defense.

But not in Montana.

Scores of ICBMs remain in their underground silos in the Great Falls area, armed and ready for Armageddon. The sites are occasionally visible from the highway, marked by a barbed wire–topped chainlink fence and a few high-powered lights surrounding an empty space. Do not approach these sites, just enjoy them from the main

★ ★

Great Falls International Airport is the current home of the world's largest collection of model planes. Bary Poletto built over 1,000 model commercial aircraft, about two-thirds of which are modern airliners. The models represent some 700 airlines, 164 countries, and 57 manufacturers.

Poletto's attention to detail is evident in the meticulously arranged airplanes, which are displayed in long, glass-enclosed display cases in

road. You don't want to get caught up in some kind of Orwellian nightmare if the Feds catch you snooping around.

But why Montana? Well, there are a number of reasons. First, the launch fuel is very sensitive to humidity, making the arid prairies an optimum environment. Also, the average elevation of 3,500 feet gives the missiles a head start, realizing a 6 percent fuel savings. Also, people are sparse.

It's a little unsettling, to be sure, when you drive by one of these remnants of such an ominous and fearful era in our nation's history. There is actually a Minuteman Missile National Historic Site in South Dakota where you can get all the background you need on these sleeping dragons. According to their Web site, a Minuteman missile can strike a target up to 6,300 miles away in the time it takes to watch an average television sitcom, thirty minutes. Well, I hope it's a lost episode of *M*A*S*H*. That might be worth it.

Silos are visible from the main highways in the Conrad, Choteau, and Great Falls area. I could tell you more, but that's classified.

the upper level of the airport. The Boeing Company was responsible for funding the new display cases when the airport underwent an extensive remodeling a few years ago.

The collection serves as an exhaustive history of commercial air travel and transport, and you can easily while away a couple of hours perusing the multitude of colorful aircraft. Poletto reportedly hand-painted and decaled 75 percent of the models.

The Great Falls International Airport is located 3 miles southwest of Great Falls, near the I-15/I-315 interchange.

Fortunately, these models are not built to scale. The collection would fill Utah.

Is This Where They Grow Those Giant Bonsai Trees?
Great Falls

Oh, those Montanans . . . they won't be content with having the longest river in the U.S. run through the state, they also have to have the world's shortest.

The Roe River in Great Falls is a lovely stretch of gin-clear water that flows from Giant Springs for 201 glorious feet before joining the Yoo-hoo-colored Missouri, the longest river in the country. The Roe

Short, pure, and clear. Like a shot of Stoli.

lies at the foot of beautiful Giant Springs Park, a popular recreation spot for Great Falls residents. It's also the location of a state fish hatchery that features a round concrete pool teeming with monster trout as big as your leg.

The Roe River's title of World's Shortest River was officially bestowed in 1989 by the Guinness Book of World Records, unseating the 440-foot, unimaginatively named D River in Oregon. Miffed, the people of Lincoln City, home of the D River (which runs into, presumably, Lake C), submitted a new official length of 120 feet, measured at "extreme high tide." The qualifier smacked of desperation, however, and in 2006 the Guinness people threw up their hands and decided to go to the pub for a pint, dropping the "shortest river" listing altogether.

Giant Springs Park is on Giant Springs Road (go figure), 1 mile from River Drive, just below Eagle Falls.

What? No Taser Light Show?
Great Falls

Ruth Garfield, Montana's first woman sheriff, never wore a gun. How did she subdue bad guys, you ask? Did she give them a stern warning and then a guilt trip? Well, you're just going to have to go to the Law Enforcement Museum to find out.

Located in the Holiday Village Mall in Great Falls, the Law Enforcement Museum offers a fascinating look at the world of John Q. Law through the years. A police scanner chatters in the background as you stroll through the collection of police paraphernalia and photos. They have ancient speed guns, old gumball lights from squad car roofs, and cameras used for booking photos.

And there are the weapons, of course, the lawman's tools of the trade. You'll see handcuffs, billy clubs, nightsticks, blackjacks, brass knuckles, butterfly knives, and ninja stars. When was the last time you heard a cop say, "Hold it right there, or I'll throw this ninja star

★ ★

Trivia

Charlie Russell's studio behind his home in Great Falls was constructed of telephone poles. This must have really angered local residents whose calls were no longer getting through.

at you!" Perhaps these were confiscated from some miscreant, martial-arts buff.

Several decades' worth of pistols are represented, culminating in a gleaming example of the Smith and Wesson .44 magnum. As any fan of Dirty Harry can tell you, it's "the most powerful handgun in the world, liable to blow your head clean off." Of course, officers of the law don't normally use such language, but they might need to get tough with some of the characters depicted in the old wanted posters and mug shots. There's also a photo of the first public hanging in Billings, in 1891, and the grim faces of various early Montana lawmen such as Hank Terrell, C. B. Schneider, and that happy-go-lucky peacekeeper, Liver Eating Johnson.

The museum is run by the Great Falls Police and Sheriff's Departments, largely from donations they receive from the public. You can donate via a functioning parking meter, which bears the sign "If you ever cheated a parking meter, here's your chance to redeem yourself." Go ahead. Put in a couple of quarters. Do you feel lucky, punk? Well, do ya?

The Law Enforcement Museum is located toward the rear of the Holiday Village Mall, on the lower floor. Their hours are from 10 a.m. to 5 p.m. The mall is located at the intersection of Tenth Avenue South and Ninth Street South.

★ ★

I Am Iron, Man
Havre

There they stand, larger than life, on the corner of Fourth Street and
Third Avenue in Havre: the farmer, the rancher, and the welder. They
regard each other stoically, with that canny Old West stare so common in Clint Eastwood movies.

But these scrappy laborers are crafted out of iron, as stiff as the
backbone of the settlers who came to carve a life out of the rugged
plains over one hundred years ago. The striking sculpture is the work
of Lyndon Fayne Pomeroy, a Billings artist whose work is visible all

"Say, did you boys see an iron mule come by here?"

over that city. The man is no slouch—Pomeroy received the Governor's Arts Award for Lifetime Achievement in the Arts in 1991.

His skill is evident upon closer inspection of the statues. Stylized and angular, the iron men are sleek but unusually detailed, right down to the fingernails. A giant wagon wheel and the farmer's plow tie everything together, and the sculpture stands in a bed of river rock in the manicured landscaping of Stockman Bank. Pomeroy's signature can be seen on the plow's tongue, indicating the date of creation as 1976.

Go ahead and get up close with these stalwart working men. They don't look like they'll mind.

The untitled sculpture is on the northwest corner of Fourth Street and Third Avenue in Havre, on the property of Stockman Bank.

"Nice House. Where Do You Keep the Clack?"
Havre

Entrepreneur, oilman, philanthropist, and businessman, H. Earl Clack was one of the early movers and shakers who helped bring the Hi-Line city of Havre to life.

After following his sister to the town in 1898 with $5 in his pocket, he worked his way up the petroleum business ladder, and pioneered the drive-in filling station. His Hi-Power brand of gasoline was sold at several stations throughout the area, from Kalispell to Great Falls. Clack's empire eventually expanded to some 200 stations throughout four states.

He sold his stations to Husky, but was quite diverse in his business dealings. His interests included stock growing, transportation, oil, natural gas, and the financing of other projects throughout the state.

Havre's most successful native son's home is on Second Avenue in Havre, part of a historic homes walking tour. It was built by Havre architect Frank Bossout in 1927, and is listed in the National Register of Historic Places.

Clack also has a museum named after him, located in the Holiday Village Mall. Named as one of Montana's 100 Most Influential People

★ ★

Trivia

Of Montana's fifty-six counties, forty-six of them contain fewer than six people per square mile. Those people are outnumbered twelve to one by livestock. This might make some people feel uncomfortable, or maybe insignificant. It makes me hungry.

by the *Missoulian*, Clack had a lasting impact on the north-central portion of the state, and his influence is still felt by Havre. When the Deaconess Hospital had to halt construction due to lack of funds during WWI, Clack donated money and time to help complete the project.

"The finishing of the third floor and the finishing of rooms was through the generosity of many friends who gave liberally, and to the generous gift of not only money but time and personal work of H. Earl Clack," said Judge C. B. Elwell, chairman of the hospital's board of trustees.

The H. Earl Clack house is located at 532 Second Avenue in Havre. A well-marked Historical Homes Walking Tour winds through the area.

Still Searching for the Fabled Oreo Cookie Island
Havre

If you're rattling around the extreme northern tier of Montana, you'll find quite a few notable curiosities in Havre, the largest city on the Hi-Line. One of the biggest of these oddities is the Milk River, which flows slowly past the north edge of town.

The milky Milk, the northernmost major tributary of the Missouri, was given its name by Capt. Meriwether Lewis, top-billed explorer of

★ ★

the Lewis and Clark Expedition. He described the river thusly in his journal:

"The water of this river possesses a peculiar whiteness, being about the colour of a cup of tea with the admixture of a tablespoon-full of milk. From the colour of its water we called it Milk river."

Sometimes you just can't improve on a utilitarian name: Round Rock. Square Butte. Big Pine. Crackerville.

The whitish color of the river is due to rock flour suspended in the waters. Rock flour, or glacial flour, consists of tiny particles of rock; these extremely fine-grained sediments are the result of glacial erosion at the Milk River's headwaters. The resulting appearance is that of a large, slow-moving river of Ovaltine.

Just don't drink it.

The Milk River runs from just north of Browning, southeast through Montana to its confluence with the Missouri 12 miles downstream from the Fort Peck Dam.

Beauty Worthy of a Palace
Havre

I have a pet theory that you can tell a lot about a town's character by its ratio of churches to bars. But when you're bending an elbow in front of the oldest back bar in the state, at Havre's Palace Bar, its statuesque beauty and elegance can really cause the line between the two to blur.

Built in St. Louis in 1903 by the Brunswick Company, the massive back bar was shipped to Montana on a river boat. It resided for a time in Chinook before Prohibition deprived the ornate creation of its raison d'être in 1919.

When the Eighteenth Amendment was repealed by the Twenty-first Amendment in 1933, the immense back bar was transported to Havre by the Weyh Brothers, and installed in the Palace Bar. Jupe Compton, owner of the Palace, reports that the back bar was actually moved from the bar's original location next door to its current

★ ★

location in a single night, because the previous owner, his father, couldn't bear to close the bar for even one day.

"You wouldn't believe how much that thing weighs," he says, recalling the herculean effort. "The mirrors are this thick," he says, holding his thumb and forefinger about an inch apart.

The back bar is the oldest in Montana that is still in its original state. It has its original finish, columns, and ornate carvings. It reaches up clear to the stamped tin ceiling of the Palace, radiating warmth from its rich mahogany and thick mirrors. There's even a stained-glass door built into the shelving. Who knows? It might be a secret passage to a church next door.

The Palace Bar is located at 228 First Street in Havre. Their phone number is (406) 265-7584.

Makes you feel kind of cheap ordering a PBR.

★ ★

And You Thought a Talking Syrup Bottle Was Crazy . . .
Havre

Rumors to the contrary, the Pancake Race is in no danger of becoming an Olympic event anytime soon. It's just too weird.

This annual exhibition of cooking and athletic prowess is a highlight of the Bull Hooks Bottom Black Powder Club's Black Powder Shoot, a family-friendly gathering held every May in Fort Assinniboine, south of Havre. Muzzle loaders, cap-and-ball pistols and rifles, and black powder cartridge guns are all wielded by buckskin-clad marksmen in some thirty-five shooting events throughout the weekend. There are also knife and tomahawk throwing competitions.

But when Saturday afternoon winds down and everyone gathers for the gargantuan potluck, the focus begins to shift to the real competitive events of the weekend: the Pancake Race and the Frying Pan Toss.

The Frying Pan Toss could not be more self-explanatory. A cast iron skillet is hurled by a female contestant (males wishing to participate must wear a dress. Seriously). Judging by the fearsome velocity achieved by some of the gals, it's apparent that they have some experience tossing out their man's dinner when he's come home late with half his paycheck gone, smelling of bourbon and irresponsibility.

But it's the Pancake Race that is the main event, and they do not make it easy. First, you not only have to cook your pancake, but you actually have to start the fire over which to cook it. Oh, did I mention that you have to start said fire using a spark created with flint and steel? Then your team's runner has to flip the flapjack in the pan as he runs 75 feet to a spot where he picks up a tomahawk and throws it into a target before returning to the starting line.

Needless to say, there's a fair amount of cheating. I was harangued into entering the race this year, and when my son got back to the starting line I saw that he'd lost the pancake en route but had cleverly replaced it with a chunk of dried cow flop.

Mmm. Pass the syrup.

The Black Powder Shoot is located at the historic Fort Assinniboine 7 miles southwest of Havre on US 87. Watch for signs, and call (406) 265-2483 for additional information.

"And on This Sacred Site We Will Build . . . a Mall!"
Havre

If you want to take a tour of one of the most important Native American archeological sites in North America, you'll have to go to a mall in Havre.

The Holiday Village Mall, to be precise. But you're not looking for the Bed, Bath and Beyond of the Plains, you're going to go around behind the mall, where you'll find the Wahkpa Chu'gn buffalo jump overlooking the Milk River. Thousands of bison bones and Indian artifacts remain embedded in the earth, right there for you to see. No glass cases, no replica artifacts, no "incredible simulations."

Discovered in 1962 by John Brumley, Wahkpa Chu'gn was excavated and developed by the Montana Archaeological Society. Today it is the most studied buffalo jump in Montana.

Three different Native American groups used the site at various times in its history. The three groups are differentiated by the markedly different styles of arrowheads they used in hunting buffalo. The Besant peoples used the site as early as 2,000 years ago, up to about 500 AD. The site was later used by the Avonlea peoples, and most recently by the Saddle Butte peoples. The last group eventually abandoned the site about 600 years ago.

The Wahkpa Chu'gn site has been on the National Register of Historic Places since 1974, and efforts are underway to have this valuable place of Native American archeology established as a National Historic Landmark.

Daily tours are offered, and a tipi marks the start of the boardwalk that leads down to the business end of the buffalo jump. Access is available during the summer months, and tours require a nominal fee.

This fascinating, unadorned glimpse into the lives of Native

From this point on lies the best evidence of Indian culture still extant.

Americans from a couple of millennia ago is easy to find. Just go to Sears and hang a right.

The Wahkpa Chu'gn buffalo jump is located directly behind Holiday Village Mall in Havre. An ornate sign at the road identifies the spot, and signs along the fence will lead you around the right side of the mall to the area. The mall is located at 1753 US 2 Northwest.

A River Runs Under It
Lewistown

If you just can't bear to leave the outdoors long enough to duck into a bar for a cold one on a bright summer day, there's a place in Lewistown where they have a little bit of the outdoors . . . indoors.

In a corner near the front door of the Montana Tavern, there's a

★ ★

chest freezer–size wooden box with a plexiglass top. Look down into the box, and you can see Spring Creek running right under the bar about 8 feet below. Floodlights just above the water level illuminate the stream, and you can see that the bar was built right over the running water.

When you first look down toward the creek, you may be shocked to see what looks like several large fish floating belly up in the stream. Relax, it's just the reflection from the variety of large mounted fish on the wall above you. Make sure you take a peek before you have imbibed too much, or you might get the idea that you're witnessing a major fish kill.

The Montana Tavern is at 202 West Main in Lewistown. To wet your whistle (if not your line), call (406) 538-9991.

Please, no fishing in the bar. Except for compliments.

Fastest Gun in the West (and East and North and South)

To say that Ed McGivern was quick with a pistol is like saying Tiger Woods is a pretty good little golfer. McGivern, of Lewistown, was the Eddie Van Halen of handgunning. His speed and accuracy helped him set several world records in the 1930s, many of which still stand today.

In 1932 he entered the Guinness Book of World Records with what was known as "the greatest rapid-fire feat of all time." At a professional shooting range in South Dakota, McGivern "fired two times from 15 feet five shots which could be covered by a silver half-dollar piece in 45/100's of a second." The closest anyone has ever been able to come to matching this feat was when Jerry Miculek managed a sloth-like time of .57 seconds.

Using his favored gun, the Smith and Wesson M&P double action revolver, McGivern was able to blow six simultaneously released clay pigeons out of the sky. He could hit a tin can thrown 20 feet into the air, nailing it six times before it hit the ground. He could shoot the spots out of playing cards and could shoot a dime out of the air. And if he happened to be on a construction site where they'd forgotten to bring a hammer, he could drive nails by shooting them in the heads.

McGivern's book, *Fast and Fancy Revolver Shooting*, first published in 1938, is still in print today. The book also discusses his experiments with single action revolvers and long-range revolver shooting, as well as his police training and exhibition shooting.

A lakeside park and statue have been dedicated to McGivern near Lewistown. Oddly, the statue is one of the few things around the area not shot full of holes.

Ed McGivern Memorial Park is on the East Fork Reservoir near Lewistown. Take MT 238 and drive about 12 miles south of town.

She Blinded Me . . . with Earth Science!
Loma

Since the demise of the House of a Thousand Dolls, Loma's number one attraction has got to be the Earth Science Museum. A treasure trove of natural wonders, the museum will keep you fascinated for hours.

This is a smallish, funky facility that packs more into the building than you could imagine. It has a real Mom and Pop feel, due in part to the meticulously hand-typed title cards and the whimsical displays. But there are hundreds of interesting, even amazing items on display, most of which have been pulled from the earth.

The floor plan is laid out in three or four long aisles, lined on both sides with glassed-in displays. They're delineated into paleontology, geology, archeology, and other scientific disciplines. You'll see petrified wood chunks from several western states, many as old as 200 million years; almost as old as the stale bagel I bought at a nearby convenience store.

A well-lit paleontology display contains various fossilized parts from a triceratops, including a rib, some toe bones, a partial jaw, and even a horn. Near the front door you'll see a phenomenal specimen, a 4-foot-long, 75-million-year-old femur from a duckbill dinosaur.

Someone (Pop, I'm guessing) has put together some highly detailed, entertaining dioramas that are a delightful break from the somewhat academic presentation of most of the material here. "Rockhound Enjoying Nature" depicts a bandana-wearing fellow, resplendent in his red felt hat, working at a pile of stones with a shovel and pick. This diorama is actually credited to three people— one painted the background, one constructed the setting, and a third built the little rockhound doll. It's obviously a labor of love, and there are two or three others throughout the museum.

One unusual display holds a number of life-size heads, each one representing the look of a human adult at a different point on the evolutionary ladder. From Peking Man through Neanderthal and clear

BUTTERSCOTCH PIE
COMMON OPAL CRUST
AGATE FILLING
RUBY RIVER AREA

This must be what the Flintstones had for dessert.

on up to modern man, each head has a strikingly real face and a full head of hair. The modish mullet on modern man gives him a striking resemblance to Nigel Tufnel, lead guitarist for Spinal Tap.

Up at the front counter you'll find jewelry for sale, as well as a small rack of dog-eared paperbacks. I'll bet they don't offer that at the Smithsonian.

The Earth Science Museum is located at 106 Main Street in Loma. They're open during the summer season. Call (406) 739-4357 for more information.

Two Heads Are Better Than One

Eastern Montana. Charlie Russell Country, the Northern Plains. The vast expanses of rich and fertile terrain underneath the biggest of the Big Sky. It's a part of the state known for its abundant wheat production, bustling cattle ranches, and dramatic, soul-stirring sunrises over the badlands.

And for its two-headed calves.

What is it with all the two-headed calves in this part of the state? There are no fewer than six museums (all right, to be fair, one of them is west of the Divide) that feature this staple of the sideshow world. Heck, at the Valley County Museum in Glendive, they have three of them. You can find two-headed calves all over the world, sure, but they seem to be especially not-uncommon in the eastern part of Montana.

I asked a rancher in Saco why I was running across so many cattle that were born with polycephaly, as the condition is known. Apparently there was a rash of them born in the late 1960s and early '70s. "That's when we started messin' around with Mother Nature," he said cryptically, looking off into the distance. I pressed him for more information, but he squinted his eyes and clammed up like Clint Eastwood in a spaghetti Western.

They're out there. Not every little pioneer museum has one, but they're the first places to look. And as a bonus, you'll see the odd eight-legged lamb. These aren't some taxidermist's gag, like the jackalope. These are mostly specimens mounted just after their short (usually just a couple of days) lives ended. One of the best examples can be seen at the American Bar in Stockett. It's a full body mount of a two-headed calf, positioned just inside the door. One look at that freak of veal and you'll probably belly up to the bar and order a double.

The American Bar is on Stockett Road in (wait for it) . . . Stockett. Call (406) 736-5601 to find out if two heads really are better than one.

★ ★

The Prizefight That Nearly K.O.'ed a Town
Shelby

The year was 1923. Oil had been discovered just a year earlier in the Hi-Line town of Shelby, and the tiny hamlet had quickly grown to a visible spot on the map. In addition to its newfound identity as an oil town, Shelby was also a popular crossroads for travelers and prospectors on their way to the boomtowns in Alaska and along the West Coast.

The movers and shakers of this whistle-stop burg decided to pool the money from all the newly opened banks to create a destination for tourists, a place where the well-heeled would come by train to recreate, see the sights, and, most importantly, spend a lot of cash.

Their first brainstorm was grandiose: bring heavyweight boxer Jack Dempsey into Shelby to defend his world championship. The bout would draw national attention, they figured, and would attract tens of thousands of fight buffs to the area, elevating Shelby's national profile in the process.

They built a huge wooden arena for the Jack Dempsey-Tommy Gibbons fight. The construction costs were financed by the local banks. Both fighters had shrewd managers—Don King had nothing on these guys—who looked around and saw a bunch of glassy-eyed wheat farmers, and immediately demanded a guaranteed payday for their fighters. The banks also fronted this money, which amounted to several hundred thousand dollars.

Well, the huge paydays negotiated by the fighters proved to be the undoing of the whole ball of wax. Promoters had to jack the ticket prices way up to cover the expenses, and only about 7,700 seats of the 20,000-seat arena were sold. Once the fight began (a real yawner that Dempsey won in a decision), fans were eventually let in for free because, well, what the hell.

The match ended, the fighters and their respective entourages left with steamer trunks full of cash, and the stadium was dismantled. In the next few months, four of Shelby's banks went bankrupt, unable to recover from the financial debacle.

★ ★

Today Shelby is a thriving little northern-tier town, where the eclectic Marias Museum of History and Art has a lively, informative display that tells the story of the disastrous boxing match that nearly sunk the town.

The Marias Museum of History and Art is located in a house on the corner of Twelfth Avenue and First Street North. They're open year-round, but have longer hours in summer. Call (406) 424-2551 to learn more.

This Man's Home Was His Castle. Really.

White Sulphur Springs

It stands on Knob Hill, looming over the town of White Sulphur Springs like a lost citadel from *Monty Python and the Holy Grail*. Its rough-hewn stone blocks and massive, conical turret suggest a medieval mansion that could contain French guards who might, at any moment, leap out from behind a wall and tell you that your mother was a hamster and your father smelt of elderberries.

But this is no Camelot, although it's known as the Castle. It was once a family home, originally built by stockman and mine owner Byron Roger Sherman. After spending a few years gold mining in Boise and running a grist mill at Stevensville's Fort Owen, Sherman and his second wife settled in Diamond City. It was there that he was able to amass his fortune by supplying miners with gear and provisions. He then came to White Sulphur Springs as a homesteader where he planned his glorious, ostentatious castle.

A quarry was located in the nearby Castle Mountains, and a sixteen-hitch team of oxen was used to bring enough material to build the massive structure. It took two years to construct, and was finished in 1892.

The family lived in the three-story stone marvel for ten years, then moved to California, leaving son Charlie to live there alone. But he soon married and moved his young family into a smaller house, presumably something a little more Joe Sixpack, a little less King Arthur.

Some people are inordinately influenced by the
nearby Castle Mountains.

Today you can tour the Castle, as well as the adjacent Carriage House. The Castle is furnished and decorated in an ornate Victorian style, and the cherry woodwork and the rockwork throughout is remarkably well preserved. The Carriage House contains a wealth of vintage wagons, saddles, tools, and furniture.

The Castle is at 310 Second Avenue Northeast in White Sulphur Springs. Call (406) 547-2324 or visit www.virtualmontana.com/montanadirectory/montanalistings/RC/montana102.HTM for more information.

index

index

index

about the author

Ednor Therriault is a writer and musician with deep roots in Montana —his great-great-grandparents homesteaded in the late 1800s in Douglas Creek near Philipsburg. He caught his first trout in a Montana stream at age five, and although he's lived all over the United States, he chose western Montana as the place to settle down.

His writing has appeared in the *Missoulian*, the *Missoula Independent*, and other Northwest publications, as well as numerous online humor sites. He also writes a popular column for NewWest.net under the name Bob Wire, the nom de guerre he uses for his musical endeavors. A guitar player and songwriter, Ednor and his band, the Magnificent Bastards, have released three CDs of "maximum honky tonk," and they play shows all over western Montana. Ednor lives in Missoula with his wife and two children.

index